LEARNINGEXPRESS

THE BASICS MADE EASY . . .
IN 20 MINUTES A DAY!

A New Approach to "Mastering The Basics." An innovative 20-step self-study program helps you learn at your own pace and make visible progress in just 20 minutes a day.

GRAMMAR ESSENTIALS
HOW TO STUDY
IMPROVE YOUR WRITING FOR WORK
MATH ESSENTIALS
PRACTICAL SPELLING
PRACTICAL VOCABULARY
READ BETTER, REMEMBER MORE
THE SECRETS OF TAKING ANY TEST

Become a Better Student–*Quickly*
Become a More Marketable Employee–*Fast*
Get a Better Job–*Now*

IMPROVE YOUR WRITING FOR WORK

Elizabeth Chesla

LEARNINGEXPRESS
NEW YORK

Library of Congress Cataloging-in-Publication Data

Chesla, Elizabeth L.
Improve your writing for work / Elizabeth Chesla — 1st ed.
    p.   cm. — (The basics made easy)
    Includes index.
    ISBN 1-57685-061-7
    1. Business Writing I. LearningExpress
II. Title. III. Series.
HF5718.3.C465   1997
808'.06665 — dc21   97-21549
                                           CIP

Printed in the United States of America
9 8 7 6 5 4 3 2 1
First Edition

For Further Information
For information on LearningExpress, other LearningExpress products, or bulk sales,
please call or write to us at:
    LearningExpress®
    900 Broadway
    Suite 604
    New York, NY 10003
    212-995-2566

LearningExpress is an affiliated company of Random House, Inc.

Distributed to the retail trade by Random House, Inc., as agent for LearningExpress, LLC
Visit LearningExpress on the World Wide Web at www.learnx.com

ISBN 1-57685-061-7

7 85555 85061 3

CONTENTS

CHAPTER | 1

Some people go into a cold sweat at the thought of having to write anything at all formal, like a memo or report for work. Others might not be so intimidated, but they still need help in getting their ideas down on paper. Are you one of those people? Then this book is for you.

WHY YOU NEED THIS BOOK

Who would have thought you were going to do so much writing in your job? Reports, evaluations, equipment requisitions, suggestions to management, letters and memos—even though you may not be a manager (yet), you end up doing more writing than you would have thought possible.

And here's the rub: your supervisor and your coworkers judge you on how you express yourself in writing. Writing probably isn't the main part of your job, but you still need to be able to get your ideas across clearly and correctly, in the form that's expected in your workplace. You probably picked up this book because you think you need help with your writing, so that you can succeed in your present job and be prepared for the next step up.

This book is for you if you:

- Have to write for your job, even if only occasionally
- Get nervous when you do have to write something
- Don't always know how to put your ideas down on paper
- Sometimes have trouble figuring out just what ideas *belong* on that piece of paper
- Get stuck with how to get started or how to end
- Can't always figure out what order to put your ideas in
- Worry about how your writing impresses other people
- Need to improve your writing skills for work or school

HOW TO USE THIS BOOK

The chapters in this book are designed to help you better meet the challenges of writing for work. Each chapter focuses on a single aspect of writing in the workplace, so that you can complete a chapter in approximately 20 minutes. If you spend 20 minutes per chapter per day, Monday through Friday, and if you do all the exercises carefully, you should become a much more powerful and effective writer (and thinker) by the end of your month of study.

Although each chapter can serve as an effective skill builder on its own, it is important that you proceed through this book in order, from Chapter 1 to Chapter 20. The first two sections (Chapters 2–11) cover the basics of workplace writing: the fundamental principles and strategies that make the difference between good and bad communication. Each chapter builds upon skills and ideas discussed in previous chapters, so if you don't have a thorough understanding of the concepts taught in Section 1, you won't get the full benefit of Section 2. This is true of each chapter as well as each section, so please be sure you thoroughly understand each chapter before moving on to the next one.

The book is divided into four sections composed of several closely related chapters. The sections are organized as follows:

- Section 1: The Basics of Writing for Work
- Section 2: Getting Your Message Across Clearly

- Section 3: Basic Workplace Writing Formats
- Section 4: Tips for an Easy Read

Each chapter provides several exercises that allow you to practice the skills you learn. Most of these exercises ask you to put what you learn into immediate practice by *doing your own writing*. Instead of merely checking off the answers in multiple-choice exercises, you'll be completing sample writing exercises. That's because the only way you can improve your writing is with practice.

No matter how many examples you see, you won't really benefit from the exercise *until you try it yourself*. Keep the answers you write out on separate sheets of paper in a safe place, so you can refer to them in later chapters of the book. To help you be sure you're on the right track, each chapter also provides sample answers and explanations wherever possible. The answers are always *suggested* or *possible* answers. When it comes to real writing, each person's answer will be a little different.

You'll also find practical "Skill Building" ideas in each chapter: simple thinking or writing tasks you can do throughout the day or the week to sharpen the skills you learn in that chapter.

THE BEST ADVICE: GET FEEDBACK

Without a doubt, one of the best things you can do to improve your writing skills is to *get feedback*. A common mistake of inexperienced writers is to not pay enough attention to their readers. However, in the world of work, a lack of attention to your audience can put you right out of business.

That's why it's especially important to keep the reader foremost in your mind at all times. After all, writing is communication—and if the person receiving your communication doesn't understand your message, you've failed in your task. By getting feedback, you can help ensure that your message is coming across clearly. Here are two ways to get good feedback.

Read Your Work Out Loud

Before you send out something that you've written, go someplace private where you can talk out loud to yourself. Then read what you've written out loud. Don't just mumble under your breath—read boldly, loudly, and clearly, as if you're reading to an audience. As you read, *listen* to how your words sound. *Hear* what you've written.

Sometimes when you read silently, you automatically insert words that aren't actually there on paper, or you skim over something that seems clear but isn't. However, when you read out loud, you can hear where your wording sounds awkward, or where your sentences are too long or confusing. You can also hear where your writing simply doesn't convey what it needs to or say what you intended.

Reading out loud also helps you get used to your writing "voice"—how you sound on paper. If you read something out loud and it doesn't "sound like you," then you should revise it. Even work-related writing should have a personality—yours—and if it sounds false to you, it will probably sound false to your reader, too.

Share Your Work with Someone Else

There's only one sure way to know that something you've written is effective and communicates exactly what you want to convey: *Share* it with someone else. Give a draft copy of your communication to a coworker or someone else you trust. Make sure your reader knows your intended audience, and ask your reader the following questions:

- What seems to be the purpose of what I've written?
- Is there anything unclear in what I've written?
- Is there anything you need to know more about?
- Is there anything inappropriate in what I've written?

Listen carefully to your reader's feedback. It's difficult to accept criticism about your writing, but you should. Critics aren't always right, but chances are if a reader doesn't understand what you've written, or sees a purpose that's different from what you intended, then what you've written needs to be revised.

THE TRUTH ABOUT REVISING

One of the main reasons people find themselves frustrated with writing is because they feel they should be able to get it right on the first try. "If I was a good writer," they think, "I wouldn't have to make changes—I'd write it perfectly from the start." They think that if something has to be revised, it is the sign of a bad writer.

But in reality, it's the other way around. If you remember nothing else from this book, please remember this: WRITING *IS* REVISING. Even the best, most experienced writers don't get it right the first time. In fact, the more experience a writer has, the more drafts he or she tends to write. Experienced writers know that they should *first* get their ideas down—however roughly—and *then* worry about making it sound "perfect."

So give yourself the freedom to write rough (really *rough*) drafts. Your goal should always be first and foremost to get your ideas written down. After that, you can refine your organization and your use of language and grammar. You don't want to worry so much about grammar and spelling that you lose sight of the ideas you need to convey. Instead, keep in mind the following order of priorities:

> **Writing IS Revising**
> A good writer doesn't try to get it right the first time. She tries to get it right the second or third—or tenth—time. A good writer knows that she needs to get her ideas down on paper where she can see them first. Then she can go back and work with what she's written to make it express *exactly* what she wants to say.

1. **Content**—*what you have to say.* Get your ideas out first!

2. **Organization and style**—*how you say it.* Put those ideas into a logical order and in crisp, clear sentences.

3. **Grammar and mechanics**—*the rules for saying it right.* Make sure that what you say is in the right format and that your punctuation and mechanics are correct. A misplaced comma can mean a misunderstood message.

If at any point in this program you find yourself frustrated, come back to this introduction and remind yourself of these basics about the writing process. Meanwhile, write well!

IN SHORT

To be a good writer, you have to be willing to revise, and often. You can find out what needs revising by reading your own work out loud or by getting someone else to read your work and give you feedback.

Skill Building Until Next Time

Write something. It doesn't matter what, right now: a letter to your mother, a request for a magazine subscription, a memo telling your boss what you really think of him. Just write. You're getting warmed up for the *real* work ahead.

SECTION | 1

THE BASICS OF WRITING FOR WORK

Most people aren't trained as professional writers, yet most of them have to do some kind of writing at work in the form of reports, letters, memos, evaluations, and the like. Sometimes writing for work can be an intimidating task, especially for those who haven't been schooled in the rules of work-related writing. Like writing that's done for the stage or screen, writing done for work has its own set of rules and standard practices. It demands communication that is logical, clear, and concise.

Did you read the first chapter of this book? If you didn't, please go back and read that chapter before you go on with this section.

The chapters in this section are designed to give you a solid understanding of what it takes to write well for work—exactly how to write logically, clearly and concisely in work-related situations. Specifically, you'll learn:

- What makes writing for work different from other kinds of writing
- How to clearly state your main idea in a workplace communication
- How to offer strong support for your main idea
- How to effectively organize supporting ideas

CHAPTER 2

Workplace or business writing has several characteristics and standard practices that make it different from other kinds of writing. This chapter will show you what those differences are as well as how to prepare for any business writing task.

WHAT IS WORKPLACE WRITING?

Why do I need a book about workplace writing? Writing is writing is writing. Right?" Well, not quite. There are actually many different kinds, or *genres,* of writing, and each genre has its own unique characteristics and rules that distinguish it from other genres. Poetry, for example, is as different from biography as novels are from newspapers. Writing in the workplace is no exception, and a big part of becoming a successful writer at work (or in any genre, for that matter) is mastering these characteristics and practices.

Genres are usually distinguished by a combination of the following five elements:

- subject matter
- audience
- purpose
- format
- style

Let's begin by looking at how each of these elements works in workplace writing.

ELEMENTS OF WORKPLACE WRITING
SUBJECT MATTER

With few exceptions, the subject of a business communication is exactly that: *business*. Though both writer and reader may be concerned about more personal or more global issues, when it comes down to it, writing *for* work must also be writing *about* work. It's that simple. Any global or personal concerns should be clearly related to the business at hand.

AUDIENCE

More than any other kind of writing, writing at work is audience specific: *What you say and how you say it depends entirely upon whom you are saying it to.* This means that before you begin to write, you need to be very clear about your audience. Who will read your communication? Why? What special needs or characteristics does this reader or group of readers have?

Much of what you read outside the workplace is meant for a general audience. Novels, for example, are usually written for a "general reader." These readers don't need to have a special set of criteria to understand or be interested in what's been written. Their desires, backgrounds, knowledge, opinions, and experiences can be as varied as the colors of the spectrum.

The readers of a workplace communication, however, are always a specific, targeted audience. It may be one person or many, but it should always be an audience that has a definite work-related reason for reading that communication.

PURPOSE

Workplace writing is also distinguished from other genres by its focus on purpose. In anything you write for work, your reason for writing must be made clear, and made clear from the very beginning. In business, as they say, time is money, so your readers don't have the time to read between the lines or play guessing games about your purpose. You must let your readers know, as quickly and as clearly as possible, why you're writing and what it is you want to convey.

This means that before you begin to write, you need to be *absolutely clear* about your purpose. What is it that your communication should accomplish? What exactly do you want to convey? And why? What should happen as a result of what you've written? Specific details about how to clearly express your purpose appear in the next chapter.

FORMAT

Just about anything you'll write for work will fall into a few basic formats, which have some specific rules for presentation. Memos, for example, should be set up a certain way, and letters should have specific sections arranged in a specific order. While formatting is generally one of the easier parts of workplace writing, it's important to understand why these formats exist, so you can make the most of them. The most common workplace writing formats are discussed in Section 3.

STYLE

Workplace communications are also characterized by a specific style. When you write for work, you need to be as clear, concise, and straightforward as possible. Remember, time is money, so there's no room for extra or unnecessary words, no time to waste on excessive description or flowery language. A busy manager is not likely to read what you write if you don't get straight to the point. If you waste your reader's time with wordy sentences, you show a lack of respect for your reader—especially in workplace communications. You'll learn more about style in Section 4, which discusses revising.

BEFORE YOU BEGIN

Just as it's not wise to go for a run without stretching, you shouldn't pick up a pen and start writing for work until you've limbered up for your task. The best way to do this is to make sure you clearly understand both your audience and your purpose.

BRAINSTORMING

Writers often "stretch" by *prewriting*—brainstorming about their writing task, jotting down ideas about what they want to say and how they want to say it. Some people get started on their writing task by creating a list of ideas to work with. However, a more helpful technique is to answer specific questions. By answering a list of questions about your writing task, you can pinpoint your audience and purpose *before* you begin writing. This leads to more effective communication.

PREWRITING QUESTIONS

1. Who *will definitely* read this communication? (Who is the *primary audience?*)

2. Who else *might* read this communication? (Who is the *secondary audience?*)

3. What *should* this communication do? What is its purpose? Try to find the verb that best describes the **action** of your message and then name the **object** of that action (the ***what***) and/or the **receiver** of that action (the ***who***). See the table on this page for examples of how this works.

Purpose	Action	Object of That Action	Receiver of That Action
welcome the new employees	to welcome		the new employees
explain the new policy	to explain	the new policy	employees
report a violation of procedures	to report	violation	management

Here are some verbs you might find helpful for describing the goal of your writing:

inform	congratulate
convince	claim
report	compromise
review	reprimand
warn	welcome
praise	pacify
summarize	impress
sell	urge
propose	demand
request	correct
suggest	mediate
remind	show

4. What information *must* this communication include? (Don't worry about the order this information should be presented in; for now, just worry about what needs to be said.)
5. What additional information *could* this communication include?

By answering these questions, you can help ensure that your communication does exactly what it's supposed to do and that its message will be right for its audience. Sure, it will take a little time, but if you brainstorm carefully, you're likely to cut down considerably on revising time. You'll also write something that effectively achieves its purpose. Knowing what you want to say, to whom, and why is the first step in writing well at work.

PRACTICE

Below are four writing-for-work scenarios. Apply these scenarios to your current job and then answer the brainstorming questions for each. The first one is done for you as an example. (Note: There is no one right answer for these exercises. Sample answers are provided.)

Example:

> **Scenario:** Your office received 40 boxes of the wrong paper, and you have to write to your office supply company about the mistake.

1. *Who will definitely read this communication?* Someone at the supply company—probably a customer service representative.
2. *Who else might read this communication?* A manager at the supply company, my manager, a receptionist or secretary at the supply company.
3. *What should this communication do?* <u>Report</u> the <u>shipping error to the company</u>, <u>restate</u> the <u>original order</u>, and <u>request</u> that the original order be <u>rush delivered</u>.
4. *What information must this communication include?* The original order (item, amount, and date of order), what I received instead (item, amount, date of receipt), and how soon I need the correct order.
5. *What additional information could this communication include?* Any information about my company's relationship with the supplier (e.g., we've never had trouble in the past), a hope that it doesn't happen again, and any inconvenience the error caused.

Scenarios

1. Your department has instituted a new dress code/uniform policy, and you have to write a memo explaining the new policy for employees in your department.

   a. _____

   b. _____

   c. _____

   d. _____

   e. _____

2. You are a manager and your newest entry-level employee (line worker, dishwasher, office assistant, etc.) is up for a three-month review. Your boss has asked you to prepare a memo reviewing that employee's performance.

a. _____

b. _____

c. _____

d. _____

e. _____

3. Your production group's equipment is old and breaks down frequently. You want to replace everything with new equipment.

a. _____

b. _____

c. _____

d. _____

e. _____

Possible Answers for Practice Exercises

1. a. All employees in my department
   b. My boss, someone in human resources or upper level management
   c. Inform employees about the new dress code
   d. The specifics of the new dress code: what exactly people are required to wear, what is and isn't permissible, when it goes into effect, what penalties people will face for not obeying the dress code
   e. How it's different from the old dress code and why it's been changed

2. **a.** My boss

   b. The employee under review, someone from human resources

   c. Report on this employee's performance

   d. My opinion about how the employee has been performing, specifying his or her strengths and weaknesses

   e. Specific examples of the employee's strengths and weaknesses; suggestions I have about how his or her performance could improve

3. **a.** My manager

   b. Others in charge of budgeting and accounting, other managers

   c. To convince my manager and anyone else involved in the decision-making process to purchase new equipment for us

   d. What the machines are; how often they break down; how they slow down production; how new equipment could increase production; specific information about the new machines we want

   e. How frequent breakdowns affect employee motivation and morale

IN SHORT

Workplace writing differs from other genres in several ways, including subject matter, audience, purpose, format, and style. What you write for work will be most effective if you have a clear understanding of exactly who your audience is, what you want to say to that audience, and why. Brainstorming and answering questions about your task before you begin writing will help you clearly establish your audience and purpose. You will also be able to clarify exactly what information your communication needs to convey by thinking about your writing task before you begin.

Skill Building Until Next Time

Take the most recent communication you received at work and move backwards. By looking carefully at how it is written and what it says, can you answer the prewriting questions?

CHAPTER | 3

An important feature of workplace writing is that it tells the reader right away what it's about and why it's been written. This chapter will show you how to clarify your main idea and express it clearly for your readers.

CLEARLY STATING YOUR MAIN IDEA

When you pick up the phone to call a friend, or when you stop someone in the hallway or on the street, it's for a reason: You have something to say. Each communication has its purpose.

But while you can chat with a friend for minutes or even hours before you get to the main reason for your call ("I need to borrow your car tomorrow morning"), you can't delay expressing your purpose when you're writing for work. The longer you wait to tell your reader why you're writing, the more you risk losing your reader's attention—which means you risk losing your opportunity to convey your message.

That's why the beginning of everything you write for work should clearly state its main idea.

MAIN IDEA OVERVIEW

The main idea of a piece of writing is different from its subject and inseparable from its purpose. If your friend calls you and wants to talk about the weather (the **subject**), you'll expect your friend to say something about the weather (the **main idea**: "Watch out. There's going to be a big storm today").

> **Subject:** who or what the passage is about (the weather)
>
> **Main idea:** what you want to say *about* that subject ("Watch out. There's going to be a big storm today.")

The main idea, in other words, is usually some kind of *assertion* about the subject—what you think or feel or know *about* that topic. An assertion is also something that requires *evidence* ("proof") to be accepted as true. Thus, if your friend tells you that there is going to be a big storm today (an assertion), he needs to tell you *why* he thinks there's going to be a big storm today (the evidence—"I just heard it on the radio and the sky is already pitch black"). The more evidence your friend offers, the more valid his assertion.

Main Idea

The main idea of a text is both an assertion about the subject and an idea that is general enough to hold the whole passage together.

The main idea of a passage is an assertion about its subject, but it is also something more: It is the idea that holds together or controls what you're writing. The other sentences and ideas in what you write should all relate to your main idea. They serve as "evidence" for your assertion. You might think of the main idea as a "net" that is cast over the other sentences; it is a *general* assertion about the topic, and the rest of what you write should offer *specific* support for that assertion. (You'll learn how to provide that support in the next chapter.) Thus, the main idea of a passage is:

- An assertion about the subject
- The general idea that controls or holds together what you write

For example:

Subject: Our current office supplies vendor
Main idea: Our current office supplies vendor *is overcharging us.*

Notice that the assertion in the main idea is *general.* It doesn't provide specific examples or evidence to prove the assertion it makes. That's the work of the rest of the passage, which should provide specific supporting evidence or examples for that assertion. Thus, the passage should look something like this:

MAIN IDEA (assertion): Our current office supplies vendor is overcharging us.
- Support: Overcharging $2.00 per ream for paper
- Support: Overcharging $1.00 per box for envelopes
- Support: Overcharging for shipping and handling

An assertion can be a **matter of fact**—something that can be objectively and systematically proven to be true, such as "A cheeseburger *costs more* than a hamburger." An assertion can also be a **matter of opinion**—something that is a personal and subjective truth that cannot be verified, such as "Cheeseburgers *taste better* than hamburgers." What about people who dislike cheese? In both cases, we're saying something *about* the subject (cheeseburgers and hamburgers).

The sentence that expresses the general assertion about the subject (the main idea) is often called a **topic sentence** (also called *thesis statement* or *statement of purpose*).

ASSERTION-SUPPORT STRUCTURE

The topic sentence is usually the first sentence of a paragraph, and it states the main idea. The remaining sentences in the paragraph support that main idea. Most things that you will write for work will be at least a paragraph long, and most paragraphs follow a very basic structure: assertion → support. For example, you could write one paragraph like the following:

People who work for themselves are very lucky. They have more freedom than people who work for someone else. They also have more flexibility.

The main idea, of course, is expressed in the topic sentence that begins the paragraph, and in workplace writing that's generally the best place for it. Notice also how both of the sentences that follow the topic sentence provide support for that idea. Thus you have a simple assertion-support paragraph.

But you might also notice that each of the supporting sentences *are themselves assertions* that could use further support. So you could expand this single paragraph into several paragraphs. Then the topic sentence of the original paragraph becomes the topic sentence controlling *all three* paragraphs—the main idea for the entire text. The supporting assertions then become their own topic sentences, in their own paragraphs, requiring their own support:

overall main idea People who work for themselves are very lucky. They have two main advantages over people who work for others.

main idea for supporting paragraph 1 First, they're their own boss, which means they have more freedom. They can set their own schedules; they can choose their own projects; and they only have to answer to themselves. They're free to take risks or play it safe, to work all night or sleep all day, and to work in a suit or in jeans and a t-shirt.

main idea for supporting paragraph People who work for themselves also have more flexibility. They can take on a variety of projects, and they often get to assume a variety of roles. If a family emergency arises, they can handle it with much more ease than someone who works in an office or factory. They can also schedule vacations, doctor visits, and so on with greater ease than someone who works 9–5.

Notice how each individual paragraph follows the assertion → support formula, and how each paragraph also supports the main idea of the entire passage. Of course, the main idea of this passage is a **matter of opinion**. You could just as easily write something with an opposite main idea:

People who work for themselves have many problems and worries that people who work for someone else don't.

MATTERS OF OPINION

In Chapter 2, you brainstormed for a review of your newest employee. It's clear what this communication will be about (your employee's performance); what you need to decide is what you want to say *about* your employee's performance. What do you **think** or **feel** about it? What is the main idea that you need to express in a topic sentence?

Your employee might be very prompt, but "Employee Martinez is very prompt" would not be a very good topic sentence because it is too specific; it is only about one of the characteristics that makes Mr. Martinez a good employee. Unless all you are going to write about is Mr. Martinez's promptness, this sentence is not general enough for a main idea.

To write a good topic sentence, you need to keep your purpose clearly in your mind. After all, that's what a topic sentence is: a clear expression of purpose. So ask yourself why you're writing.

Are you writing:
- To praise the employee for work well done?
- To report that the employee's work is average and to suggest that he or she get further training?
- To complain that your employee's performance is not up to par and suggest that he or she be replaced as soon as possible?

If you can clearly establish your purpose, then it becomes easy to form a sentence that clearly expresses your main idea. Your main idea will immediately inform your reader what you *think* or how you *feel* about your subject. And it won't be too specific. Then your reader will also know what to expect in the rest of your communication: support for your claim. For example:

Purpose:	to praise Ms. Calamari for being an excellent assistant
Topic sentence:	I'm happy to report that Ms. Calamari has proven to be an excellent assistant.
Readers expect:	to see evidence that Ms. Calamari is an excellent assistant

MATTERS OF FACT

Topic sentences for matters of fact are slightly different from topic sentences for matters of opinion. In these situations, what you think or feel about the subject is not what's important but rather **what you know** about it or **why it's important** to the reader. A topic sentence that is a matter of fact is something that can be objectively proven to be true. It is not an opinion about something. But factual topic sentences are still formed the same way as opinion topic sentences and still express something about the subject:

Topic:	new uniform policy
Audience:	all employees in production department
Purpose:	inform employees about the new uniform policy and when it begins
Topic sentence:	A new dress code for all employees will go into effect beginning on the first of the month.
Readers expect:	to hear details about this new dress code

This topic sentence is clear but general—there's still plenty of room for specific supporting paragraphs to describe this policy in detail, which is what readers expect the following paragraphs to do. It is a **fact** that the new dress code will go into effect, not a matter of opinion.

PRACTICE

Keeping in mind your audience and purpose, write clear topic sentences for the following. Don't worry; there's no one right answer for these questions.

1. *Topic:* annual Employee Satisfaction Survey
   Audience: all employees
   Purpose: convince employees to fill out the survey (matter of opinion)

   Topic sentence:

2. *Topic:* recent employee accident
   Audience: safety manager
   Purpose: to explain what caused the accident (matter of fact)

   Topic sentence:

3. *Topic:* changes in the tuition reimbursement policy
   Audience: all full-time employees
   Purpose: to inform them of changes in the tuition reimbursement policy (matter of fact)

   Topic sentence:

4. *Topic:* new automatic time sheets
   Audience: payroll manager
   Purpose: to evaluate the usefulness of the new time sheets (matter of opinion)

   Topic sentence:

Possible Answers for Practice Exercises

1. It is important that you fill out the annual Employee Satisfaction Survey.
2. The recent accident on the production floor was caused by violation of safety procedures.
3. There have been several changes to the tuition reimbursement policy.
4. The new automatic time sheets make submitting time sheets much easier.

IN SHORT

Whenever you write something at work, you should clearly express your main idea in a topic sentence at the beginning of the first paragraph. Then, readers will know right away not only what your communication is about, but also what you want to say about that subject. Whether your main idea is a matter of opinion or a matter of fact, it should be stated clearly. It should also be general enough to encompass all of the specific supporting paragraphs that follow it.

Skill Building Until Next Time

As you go throughout your day, choose various subjects and form topic sentences about them. Your subjects can be anything—your work area, your car, or the weather. Form general topic sentences for which you could provide sufficient "evidence."

CHAPTER | 4

If you want what you write for work to have maximum impact, you need to provide strong support for your main idea. This chapter will give you several strategies for providing that support and for organizing your supporting ideas.

CLEARLY SUPPORTING YOUR MAIN IDEA

Sam Meister wants a raise. He walks into his boss's office, says "I think I deserve a raise," and walks out. Ella Sanders also wants a raise. She walks into her boss's office and says: "I think I deserve a raise. I've been a reliable employee for three years; I've never missed a day of work; I have excellent evaluations; and I came up with the idea for the employee awards that have increased production."

Ella is more likely to get a positive response than Sam, of course, because she's **supported** her request for a raise with reasons why she should get one. The need for specific support seems obvious from the example above, but what seems so clear here is something that people often forget when it comes down to actually writing.

Whenever you're writing for work, if you want your main idea to be taken seriously, you need to support what you say. This support can come from one or more of the following:

- details
- reasons
- examples
- results
- definitions
- comparisons
- quotations or expert opinion
- statistics
- descriptions
- anecdotes (experiences)
- other types of support or evidence

SUPPORT FOR MATTERS OF FACT

Support for matters of fact can come from a variety of sources. One example was shown in an exercise in Chapter 2 where you were supposed to inform all employees about the changes in the tuition reimbursement program. Your topic sentence might have been something like this:

There have been several changes to the tuition reimbursement program.

What kind of support should you offer for this statement of fact? The most important thing for you to do is to tell readers how the program has changed. So, first and foremost, you must provide:

Details: What exactly are the changes?

If you tell your readers how the program has changed, then you've covered the most important information. Careful writers, however, understand that their readers will want to know *why* those changes have been made and *how* they will be affected by those changes. Readers also like clear comparisons—they don't want to have to look up a detail from the old policy to see how the new policy is different. Thus, a strong memo would also offer support in the form of:

Reasons:	Why have these changes been made?
Examples:	What might this mean in practical terms for the average employee?
Comparisons:	How does this compare to the old program?

With these four types of support, the most logical approach would be to provide a detail (a change), the reason for that change, a specific example, and a comparison (though not necessarily in that order), and then move on to the next change. Thus the support for the main idea is provided by the details (the changes), and each detail (each change) is supported by reasons, examples, and comparisons, giving readers three strong supporting paragraphs. Here's an outline of this strategy:

1. Detail: Change 1
   a. Reason
   b. Example
   c. Comparison

2. Detail: Change 2
   d. Reason
   e. Example
   f. Comparison

3. Detail: Change 3
   g. Reason
   h. Example
   i. Comparison

Assume that the three changes in the tuition reimbursement policy are in the following areas:
1. *When* you must apply for reimbursement
2. *How much* you will be reimbursed
3. *How* you will be reimbursed

According to this outline, here's how one paragraph might look:

detail—
the change—
and the paragraph's
topic sentence

comparison

reason

example

To receive tuition reimbursement, you must now apply for reimbursement at least two weeks before you register for the class . In the past, it was possible to apply for reimbursement up until the end of the semester, but this enabled employees to register for non–work-related classes that cannot be reimbursed under company policy. Thus, if you wish to register on September 1st, you must now submit your application for reimbursement no later than August 17th.

PRACTICE A

Make up specific comparisons, reasons, and examples to write a supporting paragraph for either change 2 or 3 listed above. Start with a topic sentence that clearly explains the change. Some possible changes might be: reimbursement at 80 percent of cost rather than 100 percent; reimbursement only for work-related courses rather than all courses; when and how employees will be reimbursed (after the course is finished; in a separate check rather than in the paycheck, or something similar). Or you can choose your own changes. The details you provide are up to you. Take out a separate piece of paper and write your sample paragraphs on it.

SUPPORT FOR MATTERS OF OPINION

To show how to support matters of opinion, let's return to the review of your newest employee. You may have come up with a topic sentence like:

I'm happy to report that Adrian has proven to be an excellent sorting machine operator.

Now you need to support this assertion. You can use reasons, details, examples, results, comparisons, descriptions, and anecdotes. To make the writing task easier, you might start by first listing the characteristics about Adrian that make him an excellent employee. This is a form of brainstorming.

1. He works well with others.
2. He completes his reports promptly and thoroughly.

3. He regularly meets or exceeds his individual production goals.

4. He volunteers to help others.

5. He is a quick learner.

These five items provide specific support for your assertion—support that's necessary if your assertion is to carry any weight.

But these five supporting ideas are really only a start. As you can see, each of these ideas is also an assertion, and for your review to have *real* impact, you should *support each of these assertions as well.* That is, you should offer specific evidence for each of these supports to *show* that Adrian is a good sorting machine operator.

So, for example, saying that Adrian is a quick learner is evidence that he is an excellent employee. Now you should *show* that Adrian is a quick learner by providing specific examples of characteristic #5:

One of Adrian's strengths is that he is a quick learner. Our former sorting machine operator took a week to train; Adrian was ready to begin after just two days even though he'd had no previous line experience. When Quincy Epstein had an emergency, Adrian volunteered to cover his shift and learned Epstein's line routine in just a few minutes. And when I gave him the machine manual to review, he memorized all the troubleshooting procedures by the end of the week.

main idea for this paragraph

support

support

support

PRACTICE B

Choose from the list of characteristics that make Adrian an excellent sorting machine operator. (You can change Adrian's position to something you're more familiar with, if you like.) Then take out a separate sheet of paper and write another supporting paragraph. Start with a topic sentence and add specific support for that assertion.

PRACTICE C

List three supporting ideas for each of the matter-of-opinion main ideas listed below:

1. Our new health care plan is much better than the old one.

   _____

   _____

   _____

2. There is a new uniform policy that will go into effect on the first of the next month.

   _____

   _____

   _____

3. The new machines have helped our group dramatically increase production in the last month.

   _____

   _____

   _____

Possible Answers for Practice Exercises

Practice A: Supporting paragraph for change #2

Under the new policy, you will be reimbursed for 80 percent of tuition costs for courses in which you earn a C average or better. Thus, if you pay $1000 for a course, you will be reimbursed in the amount of $800. The company is no longer able to offer 100 percent reimbursement due to the strains on its budget from opening a new office.

Practice B: Supporting paragraph for characteristic #3

If Adrian is a sorting machine operator: Adrian regularly meets or exceeds production goals. He works steadily and swiftly throughout the day. He won't take lunch until he's hit the halfway mark. He is the top producer in his group with an average of 20 units over goal each week.

If Marcelle Dubois is a custodian: Marcelle does her work efficiently and effectively. Many times Marcelle has finished her cleaning rounds early enough to help others or to work on backlogged projects. She works quickly but thoroughly; I've checked several times and found she cleaned not only to standard, but above standard.

Practice C

The new health plan is better than the old one:
1. There is only a $200 deductible rather than $400.
2. We can use any doctor; we aren't restricted in whom we can choose.
3. Eye care and dental care are covered under this plan; they weren't included in the old one.

There is a new uniform policy that will go into effect on the first of the month.
1. Beginning on May 1, all employees will be required to wear black pants of any material except leather or denim.
2. Employees will also be required to wear black rubber-soled shoes with no higher than a 2" heel.
3. Anyone with hair that reaches the shoulders must wear a hairnet.
4. No t-shirts or tank tops are permitted.

The new machines have helped our group dramatically increase production in the last month.
1. The new machines are faster.
2. The new machines require less physical activity from assemblers who therefore have more energy and move faster.
3. The new machines are more reliable, and so far we've had only one hour of downtime for minor repairs.

IN SHORT

Support for main ideas—whether they're matters of fact or matters of opinion—can come from a number of sources. Use details, reasons, comparisons, examples and more to show readers that your assertions are valid.

Skill Building Until Next Time

Make assertions as you go through your day and create supporting ideas for them. Your assertions can be about anything—from "I have a really great job" to "Ray's Slice has the best pizza in town"—and your support should show how or why that assertion is valid.

CHAPTER 5

When you write for work, it's important that your ideas are arranged logically. This chapter discusses the major organizing strategies and types of transitions that you can use to organize your ideas.

ORGANIZING YOUR IDEAS

Imagine that you've just bought your first automatic coffee machine. Inside the box are instructions that look like this:

1. Place the filter in the brown filter basket.
2. Rinse the coffee pot after use.
3. Pour water in the top vent.
4. Plug in the coffee maker.
5. Place measured coffee grinds in the filter.
6. Press the "on" button, located at the base of the machine.
7. Fill the pot with water. USE COLD WATER ONLY.

Oh boy. Obviously, there's a problem here: These instructions aren't organized logically. The steps are out of order, and the result will be confused readers. . . and lousy coffee.

Organizing your ideas can be a challenge, but when you write for work, a logical organization is essential. You can organize your ideas by presenting your main idea and its support in an order that makes good sense to your reader. There are many different organizing strategies that you can use. Your task is to choose the one that makes the most sense for the information you want to convey.

Get Organized!

Organizing strategies often work hand in hand—that is, writers may use more than one strategy at a time. One strategy, however, will generally serve as the overall organizing strategy in a piece of writing.

ORGANIZING STRATEGIES

You'll want to have a variety of options when you sit down to write, so read on to learn about the most common organizing strategies.

CHRONOLOGICAL/SEQUENTIAL

You can put your ideas in the order in which they did happen, should happen, or will happen.

This is one of the most common organizing principles used in writing at work. Whenever you report on something that happened or tell somebody how to do something, you use this organizational structure.

The most important thing to remember here is that your items *must be in the proper order.* As the opening set of instructions about making coffee show, poor chronology or bad sequencing can cause a great deal of confusion (and, depending upon what you're writing, it may even endanger your readers).

PRACTICE A

Here are the instructions for the coffee machine. Put them in the proper order—the order in which they should happen. Answers are at the end of the chapter.

1. Place the filter in the brown filter basket.
2. Rinse the coffee pot after use.
3. Pour water in the top vent.

4. Plug in the coffee maker.
5. Place measured coffee grinds in the filter.
6. Press the "on" button, located at the base of the machine.
7. Fill the pot with water. USE COLD WATER ONLY.

CAUSE AND EFFECT

Another way to organize your ideas is by showing either:

1. **Cause/effect**: what happened (cause) and what happened as a result (effect)
2. **Effect/cause**: what happened (effect) and why it happened (cause)

This is another organizing principle that uses time to organize ideas by moving from the past (the cause) to the present (the effect) or the present (the effect) to the past (cause). For example, you might say "Because Thompson didn't follow safety procedures, he therefore had an accident and is applying for worker's compensation." This moves from the past cause to the present effect.

Or you could reverse it: "Thompson had an accident and is applying for worker's compensation, but his accident was due to his not following safety procedures." This version moves from present effect to past cause. (If we're looking at something historical, both the cause and effect will be in the past, but the cause will still have happened before the effect.) You can also move from the present (the cause) to the future (the effect) if you're making predictions: "If workers don't follow safety procedures, more accidents are likely to happen."

A cause and effect paragraph might look something like this:

Yesterday's accident was caused by a failure to follow proper safety procedures. First, Thompson failed to position the ladder properly. Second, he was carrying several tools in his pockets, not on a tool belt. Third, he tried to reach beyond the safe field of extension for ladder work instead of climbing down the ladder to reposition it. Thus, when he reached too far, one of his tools fell from his pocket, he grabbed for it, and the ladder, which was not secure, toppled.

Notice the cause/effect sequence at work in this paragraph. One by one, the things Thompson did (or did not do) led up to his accident.

(Notice also how the first sentence expresses the main idea. It's a good example of a topic sentence.) You can also see that this paragraph uses both cause and effect and chronological sequence as methods of organization.

Whenever you sit down to write about cause and effect, keep in mind that most events have more than one cause and that most actions generate more than one effect. Thompson's accident, for example, was caused by several things working together, not by one item alone.

PRACTICE B

Arrange the following items in cause and effect order:

- Several employees complained.
- The time sheets were misplaced.
- The checks were late.
- The payroll information didn't get input into the system on time.

The answer is at the end of the chapter.

SPATIAL

Ideas can be organized according to spatial principles: from top to bottom, from side to side, from inside to outside, and so on.

This organizing principle is particularly useful when you are describing an item or a place. For example, if you were asked to describe the room where Thompson's accident occurred, you could describe it from top to bottom—describe the ceiling, then the walls, and then the floor. Or you could describe the room by halves or sides—what's on the right side of the room (top to bottom or bottom to top) and what's on the left side. In describing an office layout, you might start with the entrance, then move left, then right. The whole idea here is to move around the space or object logically—that is, don't jump around. Notice the difference in these two paragraphs, only one of which is organized logically:

In the center of the office is a giant desk. To the right of the couch is a cabinet. Next to the desk, against the right wall, is a couch. In the lower left corner is a bookshelf. To the left of the cabinet on the front wall is a large painting. In the middle of the left side is a potted plant.

In the center of the office is a giant desk. Next to the desk, against the right wall, is a couch. To the right of the couch is a cabinet. To the left of the cabinet is a large painting. In the middle of the left side is a potted plant, and in the lower left corner is a bookshelf.

Clearly the first version has no organizing principle; the readers have to jump all around the office as they read the paragraph. The second version, however, moves from the center of the room to the right, to the front, to the left, and back. It makes much more sense and is easier to follow.

PRACTICE C

Arrange the following descriptive comments of a small factory facility in a logical spatial order. One possible answer is at the end of the chapter.

- Behind the lobby is the employee lounge and cafeteria.
- A gravel path leads from the gate to the factory.
- Human Resources and Accounting are to the left of the lobby.
- The production floor is at the rear.
- The entrance opens into a large lobby.
- The factory is surrounded by a tall iron gate.
- The president, vice president, and managers have their offices to the right of the lobby.

ANALYTICAL/CLASSIFICATION

Some writers organize ideas according to the parts or functions of an item, idea, or event.

If an alien landed in your backyard, how would you describe it? One logical thing to do would be to break it down into its parts. You might begin with its head (or heads), then its torso (if it has one), and then its appendages (legs, arms, tentacles, and whatever else may be attached to its body). Similarly, if you had to describe your job, you might break it down into its various parts: As a team leader, for example, you might report to management, direct your team, and work on the line. All of your duties fall into these three categories, which you might describe like this:

As a team leader, I have three main functions: to report to management, to direct my team, and to work on the production line. Each week I meet with management and submit production reports for my team along with individual reports for each team member. I also report any accidents or incidents involving team members as well as any safety hazards in our area.

As a leader, I guide my team each day by reminding them of production goals and checking their progress throughout the day. I also remind them of safety procedures, offer suggestions for greater productivity, and handle any problems that arise between members or with the machinery.

Finally, a large portion of my time is also spent alongside my teammates on the production line. I rotate from task to task to check on the machines and to give team members breaks throughout the day.

PRACTICE D

On a separate sheet of paper, break down the following items into parts or functions:
1. Your office building
2. Days of the year
3. Your job

Sample answers are at the end of the chapter.

ORDER OF IMPORTANCE

You can rank supporting ideas from most important to least important, or vice versa.

Let's return again to describing an office. The parts of an office can be organized spatially and analytically, and also by order of importance. For example, you could begin by describing the president's office, then the vice president's, then the junior vice president's, and on down the line to the workstation of the lowest-ranking employee. Or you could begin with the production floor, since that's where the product actually gets made, and move on to the areas that have less and less to do with actual production of the company's product.

When organizing ideas this way, you need to keep in mind what ideas will be most important to your readers and which ideas are most supportive of your main idea. Often, you'll want to start with the least important and move to the most important. This is especially true when you are building an argument, as in the following example:

> Switching to a concentrated cleaner would benefit the company in several ways. First, it would be easier to transport cleaning equipment from job to job. Second, it would increase the availability of storage space, which is badly needed. Third, concentrated cleaners are more cost effective.

Here, the first supporting idea is good; the second is stronger; and the third, cost effectiveness, is the strongest. However, if you aren't building an argument, or if you think readers might not read all of what you've written, you should reverse the order. That way, your most important idea is the first and therefore most likely to be seen by readers. Here's an example:

> Please attend the union meeting on November 21. Delegates will be discussing proposed changes in our earnings and benefits. We will also elect a new secretary and discuss suggestions for a new meeting location.

Notice how this paragraph starts with the most important item on the agenda at the meeting. If this were a least-to-most-important paragraph, attendance at the meeting might not be as close to the beginning of the paragraph. Busy people often don't read beyond the first line or two of a paragraph.

PRACTICE E

Arrange the following ideas in order of importance. You must determine which order (most → least or least → most) is best for the situation. A sample answer is at the end of the chapter.

Topic sentence: Employees in my department have several concerns about the new tuition reimbursement policy.
- It limits the type of courses employees can take.
- It cuts the reimbursement from 100% to just 50%.

- It delays reimbursement until after the completion of the semester, requiring employees to wait several months before they are reimbursed for their expenses.
- It requires a lot more paperwork.

COMPARE AND CONTRAST

Using the organizing strategy of *comparing* and *contrasting* shows the similarities and/or differences between two or more items.

The first step to a good compare and contrast structure is to make sure you're using comparable elements. You can't, for example, compare the *height* of A to the *weight* of B. Once you have comparable elements for A and B (for example, 1–cost, 2–availability, 3–efficiency), then there are two ways to organize your discussion: the block technique and the point-by-point technique.

Block Technique

Organize by item (A and B). Discuss all of the elements of A first (A1, A2, A3) and then discuss all of the elements of B (B1, B2, B3). The result is two "blocks"—a section on A, and a section on B.

Point-by-Point Technique

Organize by element (1, 2, 3). Discuss both A and B, element by element, so your result is a point-by-point comparison: A1, B1; A2, B2; A3, B3.

Here's an example of using both techniques to compare the old and new health care plans:

Block technique:

The new health plan is better than the old one. The old plan required a $400 deductible; this plan only requires $200. With the old plan, we could only choose from doctors who were within the plan. The new plan lets us choose whomever we like. Finally, the new plan covers both eye and dental care, neither of which were covered by the old plan.

Point-by-point technique:

The new health plan is better than the old one. The old plan required a $400 deductible, and it limited us to doctors within the plan. It didn't include eye care or dental care, either. The new plan, on the other hand, has a deductible of only $200, and we can choose any doctors we like, regardless of whether or not they're part of the plan. It also covers both eye care and dental care.

PRACTICE F

Make a list of three things to compare and contrast between your previous job and your current job. Arrange these items in a compare and contrast format using either the block or point-by-point technique.

1. _____

2. _____

3. _____

PROBLEM/SOLUTION

Another way to organize your writing is to identify the problem and then offer a solution or solutions.

This is a very common and very basic format. Here's an example:

A number of security guards have complained that their new uniforms don't fit comfortably. Would it be possible to bring in a tailor to adjust the uniforms? If the tailor were on premises just one day for measurements, these complaints could be quickly eliminated.

Unlike other formats, which can be flexible, there's little room for change in this structure. The problem must come first so that readers understand what problem the solution solves.

PRACTICE G

On a separate sheet of paper, write a short problem-solution paragraph for something happening at work.

USE OF TRANSITIONS

In writing, transitions are the words and phrases used to move from one idea to the next. They show the relationship between ideas. Using transitions will help your words flow smoothly, and enable readers to see clearly how to connect your ideas. For instance, what's wrong with this paragraph?

Your ideas are organized. You have to make sure they're well connected. Readers can move smoothly from one idea to the next.

It sounds rather choppy, doesn't it? It's a little difficult to follow, too.

The problem is not that the ideas are unclear; it's that the *relationships between the ideas* are unclear. That's because this paragraph lacks **transitions**.

Notice the difference that transitional words and phrases make in that choppy paragraph above:

<u>Now that</u> your ideas are organized, you have to make sure they're well connected. <u>Then</u> readers can move smoothly from one idea to the next.

Simply by adding "now that" and "then"—and connecting two of the sentences—you have a much smoother paragraph.

Certain transitional words and phrases are particularly good for certain organizational strategies. When you've organized something chronologically, for example, words like "then," "next," "before," and so on are the most helpful. Below is a list of many transitional words and phrases and what they're most often used for.

ORGANIZING PRINCIPLE	TRANSITIONAL WORDS AND PHRASES
order of importance	more importantly, moreover, in addition,furthermore, above all, certainly; first, second, third, etc.; first and foremost
chronological	then, next, later, before, after, during, while, as, when, afterwards, since, until; first, second, third, etc.
spatial	beside, next to, along, around, above,below, beyond, behind, in front of, under, near
cause and effect	therefore, because, as a result, so, since, thus, consequently, accordingly, hence, then
compare	likewise, similarly, like, in the same way
contrast	on the other hand, however, on the contrary, unlike, but, yet, nevertheless,rather, instead, whereas, although

Other helpful transitional words and phrases include these:

IF YOU WANT TO	USE THESE TRANSITIONAL WORDS AND PHRASES
introduce an example	for example, for instance, that is, in other words, in particular, specifically, in fact, first of all
show addition	and, in addition, also, again, moreover, furthermore
show emphasis	indeed, in fact, certainly
acknowledge another point of view	although, though, granted, despite, even though

PRACTICE H

Look at the sentences from Practice B, E, and F. On a separate sheet of paper, rewrite them into paragraphs and use transitional words and phrases to connect your ideas. Some sample answers are at the end of the chapter.

Possible Answers for Practice Exercises

Practice A

1. Plug in the coffee maker.
2. Place the filter in the brown filter basket.
3. Place measured coffee grinds in the filter.
4. Fill the pot with water. USE COLD WATER ONLY.
5. Pour water in the top vent.
6. Press the "on" button, located at the base of the machine.
7. Rinse the coffee pot after use.

Practice B

1. The time sheets were misplaced.
2. The payroll information didn't get input into the system on time.
3. The checks were late.
4. Several employees complained.

Practice C

1. The factory is surrounded by a tall iron gate.
2. A gravel path leads from the gate to the factory.
3. The entrance opens into a large lobby.
4. Human Resources and Accounting are to the left of the lobby.
5. The president, vice president, and managers have their offices to the right of the lobby
6. Behind the lobby is the employee lounge and cafeteria.
7. The production floor is at the rear.

Practice D

1. Your office building: areas of "blue collar" work and areas of "white collar" work; public areas and private offices; production areas and paperwork areas; financial, management, clerical, production, and maintenance areas; and so on.

2. Days of the year: seasons, months, weeks, workdays and vacation days; week days and weekends, and so on.
3. Your job: answers will vary. Perhaps one part of your job is sorting, one part is carrying, and one part is managing inventory.

Practice E

Answers will vary, depending upon what issues are most important to you. Several employees may say their biggest concern is that the reimbursement is cut by half, and their second biggest concern is that they are limited in what courses they can take to be reimbursed. Since they're concerned that their complaint may be overlooked, they've started with the most important point:

*   It cuts the reimbursement from 100% to just 50%.
*   It limits the type of courses employees can take.
*   It delays reimbursement until after the completion of the semester, requiring employees to wait several months before they are reimbursed for their expenses.
*   It requires a lot more paperwork.

Practice F

Answers will vary. You might compare job duties, location, and salary, for example.

Practice G

Answers will vary. Just be sure that your paragraph moves from a clearly stated problem to a clearly stated solution.

Practice H

1. Practice B: **Because** the time sheets were misplaced, the payroll information didn't get input into the system on time. **As a result**, the checks were late, **and** several employees complained.
2. Practice E: **First and foremost**, the new policy cuts the reimbursement from 100% to just 50%. **Second**, it limits the type of courses employees can take. **Third**, it delays reimbursement until after the completion of the semester, requiring employees to wait several months before they are reimbursed for their expenses. **Finally**, it requires a lot more paperwork.

3. Practice F: At my last job, I worked in a copy room crowded with a large reproduction staff and a dozen fax and copy machines. At my new job, **however**, I have a small office next to the copy/fax room where I can do my paperwork in peace and quiet. My previous job compensated me well per hour, **but** I didn't get paid for holidays and I had limited benfits. Now I have a yearly salary **rather than** an hourly wage and have a paid vacation. **But** the biggest difference is in my responsibilities. At my previous job, I had very few responsibilities. I copied or faxed whatever was put in the "in" box and logged out the work I completed. My new job, **on the other hand**, entails a lot more responsibility. Now I supervise a small team of "document managers," and I am responsible for making sure all documents are logged in, logged out, and processed properly.

(Notice that this paragraph is arranged both by the compare and contrast point-by-point technique and by order of importance.)

IN SHORT

There are several organizing strategies you can choose from to arrange your ideas logically. And you will often use more than just one. Be sure to connect your ideas with strong transitional words and phrases so that your reader can move smoothly from one idea to the next.

Skill Building Until Next Time

Take an article from a newspaper or something that was written for work. Circle all the transitional words and phrases you can find. Then see if you can identify the main organizing strategy.

SECTION | 2

GETTING YOUR MESSAGE ACROSS CLEARLY

Although workplace writing may take a variety of forms and cover a wide range of subjects, its function usually falls into one of six major categories:

1. Reporting
2. Asking, acknowledging, informing: conveying a positive or neutral message
3. Complaining, correcting, rejecting: conveying a negative or unpleasant message

4. Explaining and instructing

5. Reviewing

6. Convincing

The chapters in this section will show you how to clearly communicate your purpose in each of these six categories.

CHAPTER | 6

Your role as a writer at work can sometimes be much like that of a newspaper reporter: you need to explain what happened, what you saw, or what you learned. This chapter will show you how to report your findings effectively and objectively.

REPORTING

There are several different meanings of the word "report," as you can see if you look in the dictionary. However, the meaning that is most important for this discussion is as follows:

Report: To give an account of something seen, done, heard, or studied.

SKILLS FOR WRITING REPORTS

At work, you will often be called upon to give an account of something you've done, seen, heard, or learned. More often than not, you'll have to put that report into writing.

Reports can take several forms, which are discussed further in Section 3. They can cover a variety of topics. You might write a trip report, an incident report, or meeting minutes, for example. For now, the most important thing to remember is that whatever the type of report, you need to be:

1. Accurate
2. Thorough
3. Observant
4. Objective

BE ACCURATE

In a report, it's essential that you get your facts straight. If you know in advance that you will have to report upon a certain situation, be prepared to take notes. Get a logbook or a notebook in which you can record information and details. Don't rely upon memory because all too often it fails. You may not remember key details if you don't bother to note them down. You also may find out later that something you thought was trivial is actually important.

When you write things down, take the time (either at the moment or afterwards) to check that you have spelled names and places accurately and that you have recorded dates, times, and other numbers correctly. If possible, verify any facts about which you are unsure before you submit your report.

Another reporting no-no is guessing. By its very nature, a report is designed to convey facts. From those facts, your readers will draw conclusions, take action, and/or make recommendations. You could be putting your company and your job in jeopardy if you submit a report full of guesses.

PRACTICE A

Record the exact date, time, and location where you are studying this chapter. Be as specific and accurate as possible.

BE THOROUGH

In any report, there are certain items you must cover: the **who, what, when, where, why,** and **how.** These are the basics in any report, and the more specific you can be, the better. Be sure that your report tells readers:

- **Who** was involved?
- In **what**?
- **What** happened?
- **When** did it happen?

- **Where**?
- **Why**?
- **How**?

For example, take a look at the following incident report:

INCIDENT REPORT

Submitted by: <u>Matthew Thomas</u>   Date of Incident: <u>1/21/97</u>
Position: <u>Security Guard, 2nd shift</u>   Time of Incident: <u>17 : 18</u>
Date of Report: <u>1/22/97</u>   Location of Incident: <u>Human Resources</u>

Description of Incident:
On Monday, January 22, at 16:32, Mr. R. Turner, a former employee, signed in at the security desk. He exchanged his driver's license for a visitor pass and put his destination down as Human Resources. At 17:18, I received a call from Maria Louis, the assistant director of Human Resources. She asked me to come to Human Resources immediately because Mr. Turner refused to leave the office and she could not lock up. I left Mark Davidson on duty at the desk and reached Human Resources at approximately 17:21. When I arrived, Mr. Turner was sitting by the receptionist's desk. I told Mr. Turner that the office was closed and that he had to leave. He said he would not leave until he saw John Francis, the director of Human Resources. Maria then told me that Mr. Francis was not in that day and that she told Mr. Turner several times that Mr. Francis was not in, but Mr. Turner did not believe her. She said Mr. Turner was waiting because he believed he would catch Mr. Francis as he tried to leave. Then I asked Mr. Turner if this was true, and he said yes. I told him that Mr. Francis was not in and that he could no longer sit in the Human Resources office. If he wished to wait, he could wait by the security desk, but he would be waiting until tomorrow morning. Then I asked Mr. Turner to follow me, and he did. After I escorted him to the security desk, I asked him if he wanted to wait or if he wanted his ID back. He said he'd come back later, so I returned his ID and he signed out at 17:30. Maria had followed us to the security desk, and after Mr. Turner left, she told me that Mr. Turner had just been fired for failing to pass a random drug test.

Notice that this report tells readers who was involved, in what, and when, where, why, and how it happened.

Report Questions
Keep these questions in mind when you need to get the facts:
Who, what, where, when, why, how?

PRACTICE B

On a separate sheet of paper, answer the who, *what, when, where, why,* and *how* questions for what you are doing right now or for what you were doing before you started this chapter.

BE OBSERVANT

One characteristic that all good reporters have in common is their attention to detail. They're observant; they look closely and listen carefully. When you write a report for work, you, too, need to be observant. A little detail that you notice can make all the difference in how (or how much) you, your company, and/or your coworkers benefit from your report. Details that you can look for include:

size	location
color	temperature
sound	manner
pattern	type or kind
tone	name
shape	brand
texture	material
time	style

The incident report, on page 51, for example, provides several specific details. It tells where Mr. Turner logged in, what ID he used (his driver's license), where he was sitting, and several specific names and times. Details like these can help in the assessment of an event and serve as important references in the future.

PRACTICE C

The next time you are in your work area, stop and look around very carefully. See if you can write down *at least* a dozen different things you notice about your work space. The more you list, the more you must call on your powers of observation and your eye for detail. You may be surprised at some of the things you take for granted and never really noticed before.

BE OBJECTIVE

If reporters start to color their articles with their own feelings and impressions, they lose their objectivity and, to a degree, their credibility. As reporters, their job is to provide the facts so that people can then form their own opinions about the people and circumstances described.

When reporters offer impressions and opinions, their report takes on the status of an analysis, review, or editorial. It can no longer be considered a straight news story or report. Look, for example, at the difference between these two sentences:

1. Mr. Turner said he wouldn't leave until he spoke to Mr. Francis.
2. Mr. Turner is a stubborn jerk.

Sentence 1 tells readers just the facts. Sentence 2, on the other hand, expresses an opinion about Mr. Turner (and not a very nice one at that). Clearly, sentence 2 is not material for a report.

Conclusions or Recommendations

Some types of reports include a section for conclusions or recommendations. If you are writing this kind of report, you should offer conclusions or recommendations that you feel are logical based upon what you've seen, heard, or learned. Clearly the recommendation of a report will be subjective, but in order for it to be valid, it must be based upon the *objective* material presented somewhere in the report. For example, if Mr. Thomas's Incident Report had a section for recommendations, Mr. Thomas might write something like this:

Comments/Recommendations:

I recommend that all security staff be notified of this incident and that Mr. Turner not be allowed to enter the building unless he is escorted by Mr. Francis. Ms. Louis was clearly shaken by the incident and said that though Mr. Turner sat quietly, she was concerned for her safety.

PRACTICE D

1. Cross out the sentences (or parts of sentences) that are not objective in the following trip report:

On Thursday, September 18, I visited the new plant in Smithtown. I traveled by car. The drive, which was very pretty with all the fall colors on the trees, took three hours. I arrived at 10:00. I met with Floor Manager Jim Martin—a really nice guy—who showed me how the new Quality Control system works. Whoever thought up this system is a genius. Then we had lunch with a line group. Lunch was lousy but I got to hear how the workers felt about the new system. Each employee had something positive to say about it. I left at 2:00 p.m.

2. Take out a piece of paper and answer the *who, what, when, where, why,* and *how* questions for the most recent work "event" for which you were present—a meeting, an incident, an important discussion, or any other noteworthy occurrence. If you can't remember some facts, try to find them out and verify any guesses. Include as much detail as possible in your answers.

3. Go over your answers to question #2. Did any impressions or opinions creep in there? If so, cross them out.

Possible Answers for Practice Exercises
Practice A
Answers will vary. You might have written something like: Friday, June 11, 1997. 8:15 p.m., at the table in my kitchen, in my apartment at 315 Sycamore Lane, Teasdale, RI, USA.

Practice B
Answers will vary. Your answer is a good one if you included detailed responses to the *who, what, when, where, why,* and *how* questions.

Practice C

Answers will vary. You might notice details such as old books stacked in a pile, rags in the corner, or the shape of bottles some cleaning solutions are stored in.

Practice D

1. On Thursday, September 18, I visited the new plant in Franklintown. I traveled by car. The drive, ~~which was very pretty with all the fall colors on the trees~~, took three hours. I arrived at 10:00. I met with Floor Manager Jim Martin ~~a really nice guy~~ who showed me how the new Quality Control system works. ~~Whoever thought up this system is a genius~~. Then we had lunch with a line group. ~~Lunch was lousy~~ but I got to hear how the workers felt about the new system. Each employee had something positive to say about it. I left at 2:00 p.m.

2. Your answers will vary, but here's an example.
    Event: A meeting.
    Who was involved? John, Christine, and I.
    In what? A lunch meeting.
    What happened? We arranged the holiday schedule.
    When? From 1:00–2:20 p.m. on Monday, December 1.
    Where? In the cafeteria.
    How? We each brought our group schedules and time-off requests and charted which shifts needed additional coverage. Then we took the extra shift requests, ranked them by seniority, and put those people in the spots that needed coverage.
    Why? To ensure that all shifts are covered during the winter holidays.

3. Note that the above example contains no opinions.

IN SHORT

Reporting is an important function in workplace communication. It requires you to be accurate, thorough, detailed, observant, and objective. Use the *who, what, when, where, why,* and *how* questions to get yourself started, and be sure to check the accuracy of your data.

Skill Building Until Next Time

Read through the newspaper and notice the difference between regular articles and those labeled "analysis," "review," or "editorial." All include facts, but some are clearly more objective than others. Notice how a regular report answers the *who, what, when, where, why,* and *how* questions and provides details and specific names, numbers, and facts for readers.

CHAPTER | 7

This chapter deals with a number of everyday tasks your workplace communications may have to fulfill. You'll learn strategies for effectively thanking, requesting, inquiring, and more.

CONVEYING A POSITIVE OR NEUTRAL MESSAGE

Fortunately, a lot of workplace writing involves communicating good news—a much easier task than handing out bad news. Take a look at the following memo:

Dear Reader:

Thank you for purchasing LearningExpress' *Writing for Work*. We are pleased that you have chosen our book and are certain that our guide will help you to become a better writer. If you have any comments, please feel free to write us.

We wish you the best of luck as you work through each chapter. Write well!

Sincerely,
LearningExpress

Not only is this letter a sincere thank you; it's also a good example of the kind of writing this chapter is all about: conveying a positive or neutral message in a letter or memo. Specifically, you'll learn about the following writing tasks:

- Informing and reminding
- Requesting and inquiring
- Following up and responding
- Thanking, welcoming, and congratulating

These may seem like a lot of different functions, and they are—but when writing for these purposes, you will use many of the exact same strategies.

THREE BASIC STRATEGIES

Three basic strategies are important for all positive or neutral messages:

1. Clarify your purpose.
2. Choose the proper tone of voice.
3. Provide all the necessary information.

CLARIFY YOUR PURPOSE

The first strategy for writing these kinds of letters and memos should be no surprise: **clarify your purpose and express it in a clear topic sentence.** If you've brainstormed, this should be an easy task. All you need to do is turn your *purpose* into a *topic sentence*, which you can then use to begin your letter or memo. Here's an example:

purpose: to congratulate Erik on his recent promotion

topic sentence: Please accept my warmest congratulations on your recent promotion.

CHOOSE THE PROPER TONE OF VOICE

Next, be sure to use the proper tone of voice. This means you need to remember whom you're writing to and use the right kinds of words and "attitude." Are you:

- A superior writing to a subordinate?
- A subordinate writing to a superior?
- A coworker writing to an equal?
- A customer/client writing to a company?
- A company writing to a customer/client?
- A company writing to a potential customer/client? (or vice versa?)

If you're a subordinate writing to a superior, for example, you might write something like:

The manager at my bank needs documentation from my employer regarding my salary and employment history so that I may be approved for a loan. Would you be so kind as to write that letter?

This is a gentle, polite (but not overly polite or flattering) request. A superior writing to a subordinate, on the other hand, would still be polite but be more straightforward or demanding, as in the following example:

I need your report no later than Friday at noon.

PROVIDE ALL THE NECESSARY INFORMATION

Your tone may be just right and your purpose clear, but you won't get the results you desire if you omit important information. Be sure to brainstorm carefully before you begin so that you don't accidentally leave something out.

Now let's look at some specific functions these letters and memos may serve and how to convey your message effectively for each function.

INFORMING AND REMINDING

The strategies for a communication that aims to inform or remind are really very simple:

1. Tell your readers what you're going to tell them.
2. Tell them.
3. Tell them why you've told them (if appropriate).

In other words,

1. Provide an opening sentence that tells your reader your purpose in a clear, general topic sentence.
2. Provide the specific information you need to convey.
3. Indicate to the reader why this information is important.

Here's a sample:

what I'm going to tell them — There has been a change in the schedule for "Bring Your Daughters to Work Day." There will now be a luncheon for all employees and *telling th* their children from 12–1:30 p.m. Please let Mickey Andrews know *why I've told them* — no later than Friday if you will attend.

The same "tell them" formula applies to reminders. Notice that there are at least three ways to begin:

what I'm going to tell them — [We are writing to remind you] [This is a reminder] [Please be reminded] that there will be a meeting with union delegates on Thursday, March 19. The meeting will be held from 4–6 p.m. in the *telling th* Red Lounge of the Wallace Hotel. Your participation as a union member is important. We will be discussing several issues that may *why I've told them* have a significant impact on your future wages and benefits. Come to ask questions and to make your voice heard. Please call Anna Zuchero at 123–4567 if you need directions. We look forward to seeing you at the meeting.

PRACTICE A

Use the "tell them" formula to write the following brief message on a separate sheet of paper: a reminder to your supervisor about the dates you've scheduled for your vacation days this year.

REQUESTING AND INQUIRING

Requests and inquiries follow the same general format as communications that inform and remind. Specifically, in requests and inquiries you should:

1. **Tell them what you're going to tell them:** Outline the general nature of your request.

2. **Tell them:** Make the specific request (kindly). Be as detailed as possible so your reader knows *exactly* what you want.

3. **Tell them why you've told them:** Explain why you need it and by when, if applicable.

4. **Thank them:** Remember that unless you're under contract, no one is obligated to give you anything. People are far more likely to give you what you want if you are gracious about it.

Ordinary Requests

In workplace writing, there are essentially two kinds of requests and inquiries: **ordinary** and **extraordinary**. Ordinary requests are those that fall under normal business circumstances and relationships—a potential customer requesting a brochure, a current customer inquiring about a new service, and so on. In the case of ordinary inquiries and requests, it is essential to be very clear and state exactly what information, product, or service you desire. But it usually is not necessary to explain *why* you want that information, product, or service; it's understood. Take the following example:

Dear Sir/Madam:

[I would like a copy of] [I am writing to request] your latest catalog. Please send it to the address listed above at your earliest convenience. Thank you.

This writer doesn't need to explain why she wants the catalog. It's understood that she wants it because she may make a purchase, and companies are usually more than happy to give you standard product/service information in the hope that you will become a customer (or that they will keep you satisfied if you already are a customer).

Extraordinary Requests

However, if you are not a potential or current customer, or if you would like something beyond the normal request or inquiry (an *extraordinary* request), you should explain, in detail, why you want that information, service, or product. After all, normal requests and inquiries have the potential to increase or improve business, so the addressee has a stake in responding positively to your request or inquiry. But this is not the case for special requests similar to those in the following example:

> Dear Co-workers:
>
> Time is money—and your time could mean money that's desperately needed for important medical research and services. I'm writing to ask for your time. As you may know, I volunteer at the Children's Hospital. Next month, the hospital is sponsoring a 5K run/walk. Will you participate? We need runners and walkers as well as volunteers to cover registration and t-shirt distribution. The run/walk is on Sunday, May 10, and starts at 9 a.m. If you'd like to participate, please call me at extension 3035. The registration deadline for participation is April 20. Please help us help children.

Notice how this special request lets readers know *why* they're being asked to do something out of the ordinary business routine.

PRACTICE B

On a separate sheet of paper, write a company or organization to request information about a product or service that would be useful to you personally or professionally. Include specific details in your request.

FOLLOWING UP AND RESPONDING

When you've met with someone about a plan or idea, or when someone has requested something from you, you need to *follow up* on that communication. For this type of communication, keep in mind the "tell them" formula we've been using so far and add these rules of thumb to that formula:

1. Begin by thanking the person for the letter, memo, telephone call, meeting, or whatever.
2. Remind the person of the highlights of your meeting or conversation, if applicable. Provide the information or items the person requested, and/or explain why you can't provide it.
3. End on the assumption that you will continue working together or with a "looking forward" or "best wishes" type of statement.

Here's an example:

Kara:

Thanks for your memo about the Children's Hospital run/walk. I'd love to participate. I can run in the race and I'll also be able to help with preparations. I'm free every night but Wednesdays to help. Just let me know what I can do. I'm looking forward to the race and to working for a good cause.

Notice how the memo:
1. Opens with a thank you
2. Provides the information that was requested
3. Ends with a "looking forward" statement

PRACTICE C

On a separate sheet of paper, write a response to the letter you wrote in Practice B.

THANKING, WELCOMING, AND CONGRATULATING

When you write to thank, welcome, or congratulate someone, you're often reiterating something you've already said in person or on the phone. But by sending a written communication, you're showing that your sentiments are sincere enough for you to take the extra time and effort to put it in writing.

For communications that thank, welcome, or congratulate, follow the "tell them" formula, with the following specifications:

1. Be specific about what you're thankful to the person for/welcoming the person to/congratulating the person for. Use exact names, dates, places, and so on.
2. For thank you's, explain briefly why you're grateful—what the person did that deserves special thanks. For congratulations, you might also indicate what a promotion or other achievement means to you. For a welcome, you might indicate how that person's arrival will affect you.

BE SHORT, SINCERE, AND ON TIME

If your message is too long, you may come off sounding insincere. And remember that timing is important. Make sure you send your thanks, welcome, or congratulations promptly. A late message may be interpreted as a sign that you don't really mean it.

PRACTICE D

On a separate sheet of paper, provide a brief note for one of the following:
1. Thank your boss for recommending you for a promotion (subordinate to superior).
2. Welcome the newest entry-level employee to your workplace (superior to subordinate).
3. Congratulate a coworker on a recent award (coworker to equal).

Possible Answers for Practice Exercises
Practice A
This is to remind you of the dates I have selected for vacation this year. I will use four vacation days in August on the 18th, 19th, 22nd, and 23rd and four days in December on the 24th and the 26th–28th. If there is any problem with my selections, please let me know as soon as possible.

Practice B
I am interested in purchasing a dozen adjustable workbench stools. Please send me information regarding the type of stools you carry and their prices. Also, please let me know how quickly you would be able to ship the stools should we decide to purchase them from your company. Thank you.

Practice C

Thank you for requesting information about the workbench stools. We are proud of our wide selection and affordable pricing. Our most recent catalog is enclosed. Should you wish to order from us, you can expect to receive shipment within 2–4 weeks. Please let me know if you have any other questions or if I can be of further assistance. I look forward to your order.

Practice D

#2, Letter to welcome new employee

Dear Ms. Swede: [I'd like to welcome you] [Welcome] to our department. I am pleased to have someone with your experience on board. Please let me know if there's anything I can do to help make you comfortable here.

IN SHORT

The general formula for communications about positive or neutral matters is to:

1. Tell your reader your general purpose.
2. Provide specific details.
3. Explain why what you've said is important. A sincere thank you or wish will add a nice touch that will help you get the results you desire.

Skill Building Until Next Time

Think about how you inform, request, thank, and congratulate people in person. Notice that you often follow the "tell them" formula. Listen for this formula as you talk with others.

CHAPTER | 8

Sometimes your work
requires you to
communicate bad news.
This chapter will show
you how to convey a
negative or unpleasant
message—complaining,
correcting, or rejecting—
in a way that will earn
(or maintain) the respect
of your reader.

CONVEYING A NEGATIVE OR UNPLEASANT MESSAGE

Imagine you sent your resume to Ratner's Hunting Supply Company in response to a help wanted ad. A week later, you receive the following letter in the mail:

Are you kidding? How could you even *think* we'd hire you? You have no experience in this type of work. Try applying for job you can actually do next time!

If you ever receive a rejection letter like this, you should be glad you were rejected by the company that sent it! Whoever wrote such a letter has to learn two important rules for writing letters that deliver bad news:

1. Always respect the reader.
2. Always respect the reader.

It's said twice because it's a rule that should never be broken. When the news you have to convey is not something the reader will want to hear, how you convey it becomes critical to maintaining a positive relationship with the reader. After all, you're writing for work, and you want to keep supervisors, subordinates, customers and potential customers, employees and prospective employees—in short, everybody—as happy as possible, given the circumstances. So bad news has to be delivered tactfully and respectfully in words that show you have given careful thought to the situation. Specifically, you'll learn about the following writing tasks:

- Complaining
- Correcting and adjusting
- Rejecting and refusing
- Reminding and demanding

The Most Important Rule

The main rule for letter writing is "Always respect the reader."

COMPLAINING

The equipment you ordered doesn't work and the customer service representative you spoke with on the phone was rude. This and other situations like it may call for a letter of complaint.

For letters of complaint, follow the "tell them" formula that was discussed in the previous chapter:

- Tell your readers what you're going to tell them.
- Tell them.
- Tell them why you've told them (if appropriate).

When you "tell them," be sure to:

1. Describe the exact product, service, or item you wish to complain about
2. Describe exactly what is/was wrong with that product, service, or item

When you "tell them why," you should:

3. Describe any inconvenience the error caused you
4. Describe exactly what you want done to rectify the situation
5. Request a prompt response to your complaint

That's the basic formula for writing a good letter of complaint. But these concerns deal only with the content of such a letter. A good letter of complaint also establishes the right tone. Below are some suggestions to help you in this area.

Don't Be Abusive

Keep your emotions in check and don't rant and rave ("Your company stinks! I can't believe you sell this junk!"). Insults and attacks will make you lose ground, not gain it. Make sure you're calm when you sit down to write.

Some people like to write a version that says what they really think. Writing down that version—and then tearing it up—provides the emotional release they need when they're angry. Then they can sit down and write the calm, measured letter they will actually send.

Be Reasonable

Make sure your complaint and the action you would like to be taken match the nature of the problem. For example, don't demand a refund for the full purchase price if you had and used the product for a year before it broke down.

USE "I" INSTEAD OF "YOU"

People tend to be defensive when you hurl a lot of "you"s at them in a letter of complaint. Using "I" and eliminating as many "you"s as possible takes the heat off of your reader so he or she can be a little more objective about your complaint. Notice the difference that eliminating "you" and using "I" makes in the following example:

Uses "you": You didn't send me the parts I ordered on time and you made me miss an important production deadline. You better not let this happen again.

Uses "I" and eliminates "you": The parts I ordered were not shipped on time and as a result I missed an important production deadline. I cannot afford to have this happen again.

LEAVE THE DOOR OPEN

Don't refuse to ever work with the reader(s). If you do, you're much less likely to get a response to your complaint. After all, why should they bother? You've said you don't want to work with them anymore. Besides, it's dangerous to be absolute. You might come back to them two years down the road because they have a product, service, or skill you need.

Now, let's look at an example of a letter that uses the strategies for content and proper tone in a letter or memo of complaint. The sentences are numbered so you can see each of the "tell them" strategies (see page 69) at work.

TO: Susan Niss
FROM: Fred Gregory
DATE: February 4, 1997
RE: Problems with soap dispensers

(1) My cleaning crew continues to have problems with the soap dispensers recently installed in the bathrooms throughout the hotel. (2) It's nearly impossible to leave the bathrooms clean because the dispensers leak, leaving a soapy mess on the sink counter. (3) As you know, rooms are cleaned between check-out and check-in, but by the time a new guest checks in, there's already

a soapy mess running down the counter into the sink. (3) Needless to say this does not leave a good impression on our guests or management. (4 & 5) Please see what you can do to replace these dispensers as quickly as possible. Thank you.

PRACTICE A

Your paycheck did not include overtime for the third pay period in a row. Using a separate sheet of paper, write a memo of complaint to your accounting department.

CORRECTING AND ADJUSTING

What happens when you're on the other end and you receive a complaint or realize that you've made an error? Much of the same advice applies for answering complaints as for writing them. Stick to the "tell them" format and keep in mind the following strategies:

1. Apologize, but don't be overly apologetic. You don't want to sound insincere or desperate.
2. Be specific about how you will correct or have corrected the problem—or why you can't do anything about it.
3. Be specific about exactly what happened to cause the problem, but don't make empty excuses. If it was actually the complainer's fault, make a suggestion that can help prevent future problems. You could say, "In the future, you may be able to avoid this problem by faxing your order directly to our manufacturer."
4. Avoid absolutes like "This will never happen again." It just might.
5. End on a positive note. For example, remind writers of such letters how important their business is, or thank them for pointing out the error.

RESPONDING TO ERRORS

Here are two memos about an error. One follows these guidelines and the other doesn't. Notice how much more effective the one that does follow the advice is:

Memo A

I have to confess that the report I submitted last week had an error. I am so, so sorry! You don't know how badly I feel about it. I promise it will never happen again. I was just so overworked—I had worked a double shift that day—and I didn't have time to check my report over before I submitted it. You know how crazy it gets when we're really busy.

Memo B

I am sorry to report an error in my report of October 3. The total number of units produced was 110, not 141. I made an error in addition. In the future, I will double check my reports for accuracy before I submit them. In the meantime, I'll see what I can to do to increase units to 141.

PRACTICE B

You received a memo from an employee complaining that his paycheck did not include overtime for the third pay period in a row. On a separate sheet of paper, respond to this complaint.

REJECTING AND REFUSING

Many people put off writing letters of rejection or refusal because it's not always easy to say "no." But like letters that welcome, congratulate, or thank, letters that reject or refuse need to be sent promptly. If they're not, the discomfort you were trying to avoid on the reader's part will only be compounded with time. There tends to be less sting when a person applying for a job knows within a week that he will not get it. If you wait a month to tell the applicant, you're allowing him to get his hopes up and think "no news is good news." The later your news arrives, the greater his disappointment will be.

The first rule, then, is to be prompt. Here are some other suggestions:

1. Begin by thanking the person for sending her resume, for offering his ideas, or whatever.
2. State something positive about the person or the situation, if possible. For example, you might write: "We were impressed by your resume," or "I am honored that you have nominated me for the position of Union Delegate."
3. Be firm, but not harsh. For example, a sentence like "Unfortunately, we are unable to offer you a position at this time" is much better

than "You didn't get the job." Likewise, "I must refuse the nomination" is better than "Thanks, but no thanks."

4. If appropriate, explain why you are rejecting or refusing the person or the offer. You might say, "We require a candidate with at least one year of experience" or "I have family obligations right now that must take priority."

5. Conclude with an appropriate hope or wish, like "We wish you the best of luck in your job search" or "I am sure that whoever else you nominate will do a fine job representing us."

See how this type of communication works as you read the example pieced together from above (notice the transitions, too):

I am honored that you have nominated me for the position of union delegate. However, I must refuse the nomination as I have family obligations right now that must take priority. I am sure that whoever else you nominate will do a fine job representing us.

PRACTICE C

Julia Faust applied for a promotion within your department but did not get it. Your boss has asked you to draft a rejection letter to her. Using the tips mentioned above, write the letter on a separate sheet of paper.

REMINDING AND DEMANDING

Occasionally (or often, if you have the pleasure of being a bill collector), you will have to communicate a warning or demand. The main rule for this type of communication is that your message must match the nature of the problem. Someone who is 15 days late on a payment or with a report does not deserve a threatening letter or memo. In fact, if that person is normally prompt, all you need is a brief reminder like the following:

February 15, 1997

This is a reminder that annual reviews were due on the 1st of February. We have not yet received your review, which is very important in helping us evaluate your growth as a valuable employee. Please let us know immediately if there is any problem interfering with your completion of this report or if you would like us to send you samples of other annual reviews to help you in this process.

This reminder does two things:
- It stresses the value of the annual review.
- It offers the employee a "way out"—an opportunity to explain why the report isn't done and to get it in without any real penalty.

A second notice, however, needn't be as friendly. Your following notices should begin with a reminder of the employee's obligation. They should also ask if something is preventing him from doing what he is supposed to do—maybe it's not his fault. Finally, your communications should give a deadline of some sort. "Immediately" or "as soon as possible" often works best if the situation is not something absolutely urgent, as in the following example:

March 1, 1997

Your annual review was due on the 1st of February. It is now one month late. If there is a problem preventing you from completing this report, please let us know immediately. Otherwise, we expect you to submit your report as soon as possible.

If, after such a notice, you still don't get the response you desire, your next communication should be less cooperative and more demanding. It's okay to offer a vague threat. If you'd like to offer a specific threat (for example, "If we do not receive payment within 10 days, we will report your delinquency to a collection agency"), make sure it's a threat you can stick to. You should also continue to offer a way out; if you don't, the person may say, "Well, if you're going to send a lawyer after me no matter what, I may as well wait to pay."

PRACTICE D

1. George Reade has been late for work 10 times in the last two weeks. Remind him in a memo (on a separate sheet of paper) that he is to be on time and warn him that continued lateness will get him fired.

2. George Reade continues to be late. It's time to give him a written ultimatum. Practice writing this kind of memo, too.

Possible Answers for Practice Exercises

Practice A

I am having a serious problem with my paychecks. For the third pay period in a row, my paycheck has not included my overtime pay even though I submitted my time sheets on time. Three weeks ago when the first error occurred, I was told by your office that the missing overtime pay would be included in my next check; it was not, and that check was also missing overtime pay for that pay period. The same thing happened the following week. I am now owed three weeks of overtime pay. This error has put me in a difficult financial situation as I depend upon this overtime pay. Please correct the error immediately so that my future checks contain the overtime pay I earn each week. In addition, I expect to receive the overtime pay that is owed to me without any further delay. Please call me at extension 548 to let me know when I can pick up my past-due overtime pay. Thank you for your prompt attention to this matter.

Practice B

We deeply regret the recent error in your paychecks. We have discovered that there was an error in your account on the payroll system and we have corrected the problem. Your future checks should include the overtime pay you are due. We have also prepared a check for the overtime pay that is owed to you. You may pick up that check tomorrow morning.

Practice C

Thank you for your application for the position of Department Manager. I am sorry to inform you that you have not been awarded the promotion. Your reviews have been excellent since you joined six months ago and you have achieved great success in your sales, but we would like you to have at least a full year of sales experience with us before you move into a management position. We sincerely hope that you will apply for this position again next year.

Practice D

1. As an employee of the second shift, your hours of work are 4 P.M.–12 A.M. Because others depend upon you to complete their work in a timely manner, and as we have an around-the-clock operation, it is important that you arrive promptly at 4 P.M. If there are special circumstances preventing you from starting work at 4 P.M., please let me know immediately. Otherwise, I expect that, going forward, you will report to work on time.

2. Four weeks ago you received a warning about habitual lateness. During those four weeks, you have been late twelve days and absent one day. This is your final warning. You must report to work by 4 P.M. every day for the next two weeks or you will be fired two weeks from today. Continued employment after that date will depend on your maintaining an outstanding on-time record.

IN SHORT

Bad news *can* be conveyed gracefully and effectively. Remember to respect your reader and to be sincere when your purpose is correcting, adjusting, rejecting, refusing, or demanding.

Skill Building Until Next Time

Listen to how people refuse, reject, warn, and complain in their conversations. What techniques do speakers use to get the response they desire? After reading this chapter, can you tell what people do well and what they do wrong in these situations?

CHAPTER | 9

Employees are often called upon to explain how to do things, both orally and in writing. This chapter will show you how to write clear and effective procedures and instructions.

WRITING PROCEDURES AND INSTRUCTIONS

Every new piece of equipment people buy comes with a set of instructions. If those instructions aren't clear, or if they're missing a step, it will be difficult to use that equipment—and someone may even end up getting hurt. Time, money, customers, your job and the jobs of others—there's a lot at stake in writing instructions. That's why it's critical to get it right, absolutely right, before giving written instructions to others.

KNOW YOUR READERS

The first step in writing a set of instructions or explaining procedures should be familiar to you by now: **identify your audience.** Who will be reading these instructions or procedures? What do these readers need to know, and why? At what level of technicality or familiarity should you be writing to those readers?

Your instructions will be most successful if you consider your audience and determine the **"lowest common denominator"** of knowledge. If all readers know A, most know B, and only some know C, you can't write to the level of B or C—you *must* write to level A. If you don't, those readers who know A but don't know B or C will not be able to follow your directions.

Writing instructions is the one time that it's okay to risk wasting your readers' time by telling them things they may already know. Readers will simply skip over what's familiar. They can quickly separate new information from old. But what you can't do is omit what someone *may not* know.

BE THOROUGH

In writing instructions or procedures, you should be as thorough as possible. With your lowest common denominator in mind, list and explain every step of the process for someone at that level. For example, let's return to the example of instructions for a coffee machine.

Know Your Audience
Ask yourself, "What do my readers need to know, and why?"

Let's say you got a new machine in your employee lounge and wanted to write directions for its use. Most readers, you might assume, have a coffee machine at home, but you can't be sure. Maybe one or two people don't. Maybe some people only drink tea and have never used a coffee machine. Thus, the lowest common denominator—the level at which you must write—is made up of people who have *never* used a coffee machine before. So the instructions will have to be detailed if you want to be sure you will always have a decent cup of coffee.

MAKE INSTRUCTIONS EASY TO FOLLOW

In addition to being written for the right audience, good instructions are also easy to follow. Here are a number of strategies to help you write directions that are easy to follow:

"SIGNPOST" YOUR READERS

Let your readers know that they're doing things right. For example, "Take Route 1 to Main Street" is not nearly as helpful as the following:

> Take Route 1 five miles (approximately 10 minutes) to Main Street. Look for the YMCA on your left; Y Street is the next intersection after the YMCA. (If you pass the gas station, you have gone too far.)

USE LISTS

Lists are easier to follow than straight narrative. Use separate paragraphs for each step, and, if possible, number or letter those paragraphs or set them off with bullets. (You'll find several numbered lists throughout this book.) It's also crucial to list the steps in **chronological order**. This is a must! Steps in a list that are out of order will confuse readers and may even endanger them.

USE SPECIFIC INFORMATION

Use exact names and numbers (times, distances, sizes, etc.) whenever possible. If you are vague, your readers may have trouble. For example, "Submit your evaluations to Human Resources" is not nearly as clear as "Submit your evaluations to Deana Brown in Human Resources, Room 112."

USE WARNINGS

You can help your readers by providing warnings or cautions when appropriate. For example, "WARNING: If the valve is not in the 'off' position, pressure build-up may cause the pipe to burst." Adding warnings can make your directions much safer.

THREE-PART STRUCTURE

Another aspect to keep in mind is that instructions generally have three parts: an introduction, a body, and a conclusion. Although these three parts appear in many different types of writing, the focus here is on structure for instructions and procedures.

INTRODUCTION

All instructions should have some sort of introduction. For a short set of instructions, all you really need is an explanation of what the instructions are for: "How to clear a paper jam" or "Procedure for clearing paper jams," for example. In this case, your introduction is really the same thing as your title.

If your instructions are more detailed, or if there's a particular reason people should follow these instructions, then an introduction should also tell readers *why the instructions are important*. For example, you might get a memo from payroll with the following introduction:

Below are the procedures for completing and submitting time sheets. It is essential that you fill out the sheets properly. Errors on these sheets will mean errors on your paycheck. Be sure to fill out each sheet completely. Incomplete sheets will not be processed.

This introduction offers important information that will help readers follow the procedures more carefully. Introductions for instructions may also:

- Indicate how long the procedure will take
- Describe what the finished product should be like
- Mention a particularly important item that might be overlooked or that needs to be emphasized ("Be sure to pay particular attention to the deadlines listed below")
- List any materials that the reader may need to follow the instructions—forms, tools, etc.

BODY

The body of a set of instructions, as discussed, lists the specific steps of the procedure *in chronological order*. The body of a piece of writing is where the bulk of information is found. The body can vary greatly in length depending on how much information is needed to follow the instructions.

CONCLUSION

A brief conclusion is often helpful for readers. You can tell readers:

- Whom to call if they have any trouble
- What to expect next or from the results
- How to follow up, if necessary, on the procedure ("If you do not receive a reimbursement check within three weeks, contact Ms. Miller in accounting at extension 345.")

BE COMPLETE

It is crucial to include all relevant information in your instructions. You may need to write out a list and then ask questions about it to ensure that nothing has been left out. For example, take a look at the following set of instructions:

Procedures for Tuition Reimbursement

1. Fill out an application.
2. Get your supervisor's approval.
3. Submit the application to Human Resources.
4. When you receive your grade for the course, bring it to payroll along with a copy of your approved application.
5. Specify whether you want to be reimbursed by separate check or have the amount added directly to your payroll check.

If you were to follow these procedures, you very likely might not get your reimbursement. Why not? Because one vital piece of information is missing from this set of instructions: when the application should be submitted. If there's a deadline for submitting that application and you miss it, you won't get your money back. Also, these instructions don't tell you where to get the application form, if that form has a particular name or number, or where you should indicate how you want to be reimbursed. Is there a separate form to fill out? A box to check on the application?

Furthermore, the writer of these instructions assumes readers know what types of classes and employees qualify for tuition reimbursement. If there are limitations, readers need to know.

PRACTICE A

On a separate sheet of paper, revise the tuition reimbursement instructions listed above so that they are more effective. Include a brief introduction and conclusion.

A FEW MORE TIPS

Before you embark on a set of instructions of your own, here are a few more suggestions:

- Always make sure you thoroughly understand a procedure before you attempt to write about it. If you don't, you drastically increase the likelihood that you will leave something out or make a mistake in order.
- Get feedback. As discussed in the introduction to this book, getting feedback is the best way to ensure that what you've written does what it's supposed to do. This is especially important for instructions.
- Before you hand over instructions to someone else, follow your instructions yourself. Don't do what you know how to do; do only what you've written, exactly how you've written it. Does it work? If not, revise. Then show your instructions to someone else, preferably someone who has never done the task you're explaining. Are your instructions are clear? easy to follow? complete? See if your reader can perform that task without any trouble.

PRACTICE B

Your company is expecting some people from out of town and you have been asked to write up instructions for how to get to your office. Write these instructions, assuming, for the sake of this exercise, that everyone is coming from your home. Remember, if it's possible that even one person has never made this trip before, you have to include *all* steps and details.

Possible Answers for Practice Exercises

Practice A

Procedures for Tuition Reimbursement:

All full-time employees are eligible for tuition reimbursement for under-graduate course work towards an AA, BA, or BS degree or graduate coursework that is work-related. To receive reimbursement for tuition expenses, **you must submit a completed application form to Human Resources *before* you register for class.** In addition, you must earn a C or better in the class in order to be eligible for reimbursement. Detailed instructions follow:

1. Get a Tuition Reimbursement Application Form from Debbie in Human Resources.
2. Fill out the form *completely*. Incomplete forms cannot be approved.
3. Have your supervisor sign the bottom of the form.
4. Make a copy of the completed form to keep for records. You will need this form to pick up your reimbursement.
5. Submit the original completed application to Lorraine in Human Resources. Human Resources must have this form on file before you register for the course.
6. When you receive your grade report for the course, take it to Jennifer or Andrew in payroll along with a copy of your completed application.
7. Request a Reimbursement Receipt form. Indicate on this form whether you want to be reimbursed by separate check or have the amount added directly to your payroll check. Give this form, your grade report, and your application form to Jennifer or Andrew for processing. (You should make a copy of all forms for your own records before submitting them to payroll.)

If you complete all of these steps you should receive your reimbursement check in the next payroll period. Please call Lorraine in Human Resources at extension 4488 if you have any questions about the procedure.

Practice B

Answers will vary, but a good set of instructions should be in some sort of list, should include specific names and numbers ("go through three stop lights and turn left onto Mulberry Road"), and should signpost readers ("The office is 1/4 mile past the large 'Drink Milk' billboard").

IN SHORT

Good instructions are vital for good workplace communication. Make sure your instructions take readers step by step through the process and that each step is explained carefully and clearly. Know your audience, and be thorough in completing the introduction, body, and conclusion of your instructions. Signpost your readers and help them along by being specific and by numbering or bulleting the list of steps.

Skill Building Until Next Time

Look through magazines to find "how-to" articles. Notice how these articles are written and identify their audience. (Note: If it's a specialized magazine, like *Gourmet*, notice that some terms, like "blanche," may not be explained because the audience is specialized and readers are expected to know specialized cooking terms.)

CHAPTER | 10

REVIEWING

If you're thinking of going to the theater, how do you decide which movie to see? Most people look for some kind of critical reaction or judgment. What did their friends think of it? What do the papers say about it? People often look to reviews (formal or informal) to help them decide on everything from what book to read to what car to buy.

Reviews also play an important role in the workplace. People, places, programs, and products all get reviewed, and because a review can help decide the fate of that person, place, program, or product, it's very important that it be written well.

Reviews, unlike reports, are marked by **personal opinion, impression, or reaction**. A review, in short, says, "Here is what I think, and here's why." What distinguishes a good review from a bad one is the "why"—how much and what kind of evidence is offered to *support* the writer's assertions.

PARTS OF REVIEWS

In general, a review should do the following:

- Make a strong, clear assertion about the person, place, or thing being reviewed
- Offer a brief explanation of why an issue is being reviewed, if applicable
- Offer strong evidence supporting the opening assertion

The main difference between a review and a report is that reporting demands **objectivity**—that writers tell only what they have seen, heard, or learned. A review, on the other hand, demands **subjectivity**—that writers tell what they think or feel about something.

When you are faced with the task of writing a review, you may want to begin by filling in the blank in a sentence like the following:

I think wearing hairnets is _____.
I feel wearing hairnets is _____.

Try to fill in the blank with as many different words and ideas as possible. Then, find the word or idea that sums up all of the words and ideas you've listed. (This will have to be a *general* word or idea so that it can serve as a topic sentence; see Chapter 3 if you need a refresher.)

The Difference Between Reports and Reviews

Reports are objective (based on fact).
Reviews are subjective (based on opinion).

SUPPORT YOUR ASSERTIONS

Offer specific, detailed support for your assertions in a review. For example, take a look at the review mentioned earlier of an entry-level employee:

I'm happy to report that Adrian has proven to be an excellent sorting machine operator.

One of Adrian's strengths is that he is a quick learner. Our former sorting machine operator took a week to train; Adrian was ready to begin after just two days even though he'd had no previous sorting machine experience. When Quincy Epstein had an emergency, Adrian volunteered to cover his shift and learned Epstein's routine in just a few minutes. And when I gave him the machine manual to review, he memorized all the troubleshooting procedures by the end of the week.

I'm also impressed by Adrian's desire to help others. When he hears that someone is having a problem, he immediately offers to help. When Jennifer was backlogged, he asked if I would mind if he spent an hour or two helping her catch up since he was a little bit ahead for the day.

Notice that this review begins with a clear assertion that shows how the writer feels about Adrian. This is also a good review because it offers specific, detailed support for its assertion.

There is one potential problem with this review, though: Because it is filled with nothing but praise for Adrian, it may make Adrian seem a little too good to be true.

INCLUDE BOTH GOOD AND BAD

A review that is entirely one-sided (either completely positive or completely negative) might not be taken as seriously as one that shows some balance. This doesn't mean that you can't write a good or bad review; it simply means you should show that you're discriminating—that *you've looked for the bad in the good or the good in the bad.*

It's rare, but not impossible, that a person, place or thing is completely negative, without one redeeming quality, or that someone or something is perfect, without a single flaw. However, if you write a rave review of Adrian and point out one area in which Adrian could improve, your review will generally have much more credibility than a review that finds no room for improvement. Your review will then show that:

- Adrian is not a robot (Adrian is human and has faults)
- You have the ability to distinguish between good and bad, between levels of service or performance

In order to make the review of Adrian more credible, then, you might add a sentence like:

I would like to see Adrian improve in one area: assertion. He is so eager to please us all that sometimes he lets others take advantage of him.

Notice how in pointing out a weakness in Adrian, you've also pointed out a strength. But you don't have to; you could say:

One area where Adrian has to improve is in math. I have caught many errors in his calculations in weekly reports.

Whatever the case, you could then make suggestions to correct the problem:

I would be happy to talk with Adrian about this if you think it would be appropriate.

Perhaps the company would allow Adrian to take a math refresher course at the local community college.

PRACTICE

1. On a separate sheet of paper, write a brief review of the last movie you saw. Be sure to use strong specific support for your main idea.
2. Write a review of your supervisor. (He or she gets to review you, so now it's your turn!) Be sure to use strong, specific support for your main idea.

Possible Answers for Practice Exercises

1. Your review might be a positive or a negative one, but make sure it says which it is up front. It should also give your specific reasons for liking or not liking the movie. And generally, you should be able to find at least one good point in a bad movie, or one thing that wasn't up to par in a good one.

2. Your review will be different, of course, but here's an example:
   Ted is an ideal supervisor. He is patient and fair. When there was a disagreement between two assemblers, for example, he listened carefully to both sides and helped them work out a compromise. He lets us know exactly what he expects from us and then if we don't come through, he always gives us a second chance. He also shows respect for us. He never criticizes us or our work in front of others and always asks for our opinions. Finally, he's a great supervisor because he understands when family obligations and emergencies interfere with work. Last month, for example, when my daughter became ill at school, he personally covered my shift so I could leave early. The only thing I would change about Ted is that he is sometimes forgetful. Last week, for example, he forgot to tell us about the change in the meeting time for the union meeting. Still, he's a terrific boss and I am very glad to be working for him.

IN SHORT

Reviewing is an important function of writing for work. A good review makes a strong, clear assertion about what the writer thinks or how the writer feels and is supported by strong, specific evidence. It avoids being completely one-sided and may offer recommendations.

Skill Building Until Next Time

Look at reviews in your local paper: restaurant, movie, performance, book, and car reviews. Notice how the experts do it.

CHAPTER | 11

Much of what people
write for work is meant
to convince others to
think or act in a certain
way. The strategies you
learn in this chapter
will help you achieve
such a purpose.

CONVINCING

So much of what people write for work
requires them to convince others to take action or approve of
an idea. Whether it's "selling" a product or an idea, or proposing a project or a pay raise, convincing is an essential workplace writing
function. The better you are at it, the more effective you will be at
getting what you want.

This chapter will focus on how you can convince others in the
following types of situations:

- You could really use some new equipment in your work area.
  How do you convince your supervisor to purchase what you
  need?

- You'd like to be transferred to another team or department. How do you convince your supervisor to approve the move?
- The charity you support is holding a benefit. How do you convince coworkers to participate?

BEGIN BY BRAINSTORMING

Clear answers to your brainstorming questions are essential if you are to write something that's convincing. Successfully convincing your readers starts from a clear understanding of who those readers are and why you are writing. Exactly whom are you trying to convince? The more specific you can be about your audience, the better you will be able to determine the wants and needs of your readers. And the more you know what your readers want and need, the easier it is to show how what *you* want fills their desires or needs.

Next, brainstorm about your purpose. Clearly, your main goal is to convince. But what exactly do you want to convince your readers to think or do? Here is an expanded list of verbs to help you clarify your purpose:

Purpose—to convince someone to:

help	call	register
send	visit	change
buy	agree	implement
do	write	permit
choose	approve	start
allow	pay	end

Many other verbs might apply, but this list should help you get started.

SHOW BENEFITS

Once your audience and purpose are clear, the next step is to clarify exactly how your readers will benefit from doing what you ask. True, people will often do things for you just because they want to make you happy. But at work, people generally need to know that there are clear work-related benefits before they will agree to do what you ask. You know how you'll benefit from what you want; now, how will the reader or the company benefit? List as many benefits as possible, even though you might not use them all.

For example, if you want new equipment—a new industrial floor polisher, for example—you might list the following benefits:

- It will save time.
- It will save money now.
- It will save money in the future.

These are three clear benefits for the company and good reasons to agree to your request.

PROVIDE SPECIFIC EVIDENCE

So you've told your readers that they will get certain benefits from agreeing to do what you ask. Why should they believe you? How do they know, for example, that a new polisher will save time and money? The answer, of course, is to provide specific evidence for your claims. To support the claims about the polisher, you might add the following information:

- New industrial polishers cover twice as much floor space as our current polisher, so they polish twice as much floor in the same amount of time.
- New industrial polishers are more powerful, so they give a stronger shine in less time.
- We would be able to stop spending money on replacement parts and repairs for our current polisher, which cost us $800 last month alone.
- New industrial polishers come with extended service warrantees, so repair costs in the future will be minimal.

ANTICIPATE OBJECTIONS

If what you want requires people to give up time, energy, or money—*especially* if you want them to spend money—they are probably going to have reservations or objections to what you want them to do. And if they are going to have to get approval from someone else, *that* person might have reservations and objections as well. You're much more likely to convince people if you acknowledge and overcome their reservations and objections.

For example, if you want to convince your supervisor that your company needs a training manual in Spanish, chances are that even if your supervisor agrees that it's a good idea, she will have reservations about spending the time and money to have someone translate the manual. You might address those objections by saying something like the following:

> Of course, it will require time and money to translate the manual. But over half of our employees are native speakers of Spanish, and many have only elementary reading skills in English. I have spent more hours in the last few months explaining things that are clearly written in our manual than a person would spend translating the manual.

Notice how this paragraph acknowledges the reader's reservation and then dismantles it by showing how its really not an issue. This is an essential component of any piece of writing that aims to convince.

REQUEST A CLEAR AND SPECIFIC ACTION FROM YOUR READER

Another strategy for effective convincing is to request a specific action from your reader. You've asked for what you want; you've shown readers exactly how they will benefit; now, as you conclude, tell readers exactly what you want them to do. For example, you might write:

> Please approve a purchase order for a new industrial floor polisher. A page from our supplier's catalog is attached.

Or:

> A Spanish version of our training manual would be very helpful to me and to the entire staff. Please approve this project.

CATCH YOUR READERS' ATTENTION

If your relationship to your audience is not a very formal one, or if the matter that you write about is not extremely serious or formal, try an introduction that catches the reader's attention. You might highlight the greatest benefit of the thing you are proposing, mention something the reader would like to see happen, make a comparison, or ask a question that appeals to your reader's emotions. For example, let's take another look at the extraordinary request from Chapter 7.

> Time is money—and your time could mean money that's desperately needed for important medical research and services. I'm writing to ask for your time. As you may know, I volunteer at the Children's Hospital. Next month, the hospital is sponsoring a 5K run/walk. Will you participate? We need runners and walkers as well as volunteers to cover registration and t-shirt distribution. The run/walk is on Sunday, May 10, and starts at 9 a.m. If you'd like to participate, please call me at extension 3035. The registration deadline for participation is April 20. Please help us help children.

Notice that this memo doesn't appeal to the reader's desire to do a good job or improve business. Instead, the memo appeals to the reader's desire to help others, to participate in a good cause (an indirect personal benefit). Notice also how this memo starts off with a play on the well known sentence "Time is money," a rather unusual approach especially in comparison to some of the standard topic sentences we've been writing.

We'll have more on this type of introduction in Chapter 16. It's appropriate only in more informal situations, such as coworker to coworker. The bottom line is, catchy introductions will grab your readers' attention and get them to read your communication. And if you've aroused a powerful emotion, readers are more likely to be convinced to do what you ask.

PRACTICE

1. There's an internal promotion and you want the job. On a separate sheet of paper, write a letter to the department manager convincing him or her to consider you for the position.
2. You want union members to vote a certain way on an important issue. Write them a memo that convinces them to do what you want. (If you don't belong to a union, create a similar situation that applies to your work.)

Possible Answers to Practice Exercises

1. Dear Mrs. Williams:

   I would like to be considered for the position of forklift crew foreman. I have been a forklift operator for 15 years and have seen everything that could possibly go wrong on the factory grounds. I have trained many new forklift drivers and for several years I lead a small forklift crew for another company. I realize I have only been an employee of Forklift United for 6 months, but I assure you I am thoroughly familiar with all the policies and procedures here, and I have already established an excellent relationship with my coworkers. With my years of experience and my dedication to the job, I would be a very effective foreman. Please let me know when I should come by for an interview.

2. Answers will vary. Your answer is a good one if you show a clear purpose, discuss the benefits to your readers, anticipate their objections, and provide specific evidence to support your main idea.

IN SHORT

Convincing requires you to show your readers exactly how they or the company will benefit from doing what you want them to do. You need to provide evidence for your assertions, and you also have to address reservations and objections so that you can overcome them. It can be helpful to request clear and specific action from your readers.

Skill Building Until Next Time

Much of the mail you receive attempts to convince you—to buy a product, support a charity, renew a subscription. Look at how these letters try to convince. What benefits do they show you? How do they address and overcome your reservations and objections? What action would they like you to take?

SECTION | 3

BASIC WORKPLACE WRITING FORMATS

Now that you know how to convey your main idea clearly and concisely and how to get across various kinds of messages, it's time to work on the *shape* of your message. Most of what you write for work will be presented in one of four basic formats:

- Letters
- Memos
- Reports
- Proposals

Each of these formats has its own rules for presentation. The chapters in this section will show you these rules and how to make the most of them.

CHAPTER | 12

Letters are used to communicate with others outside your company and for official correspondence within your company. This chapter will show you the parts of such letters and the most common formats for them.

LETTERS

Often what people say in a workplace letter is something that could have been said in person or on the phone. But if it's something important—something that they'll want to refer to or reference later; something that involves money, contracts or obligations; or something that they'll want to have proof of having said or done—it must be put in writing. That's why most correspondence with others outside the company is in the form of a standard business letter.

Chapters 6–11 discussed the various functions a letter or other communication may have—requesting, reminding, reviewing, convincing, and so on. This chapter shows you the specific formats those letters may have.

Letters follow a certain format for two reasons:

- To provide readers with certain necessary information (who wrote to whom, when, and about what)
- To help organize information neatly

In addition, because business letters have followed a certain format for so long, readers automatically know where to look to find certain information, so following the established format makes your letters reader-friendly.

A WORD ABOUT NEATNESS

In letters written at work, *how you present what you say* often matters as much as *what you say*. A reader who receives a sloppy letter with typographical errors, stray pen marks, and text that runs off the bottom of the page may be tempted to throw the letter out without even reading it.

Neatness Counts

Give a good first impression of your letter by ensuring it has no typos, it is centered properly on the page, and the paragraphs do not look crowded.

When you're writing at work, neatness counts—and it counts for quite a lot. Readers will form an opinion of you and your company simply from the appearance of your letter, and this can make all the difference in how seriously your readers treat what you have to say.

If a letter of recommendation is sloppy, for example, it will undermine that recommendation. And that's not fair to the person who's being reviewed in the letter. Sloppy typing and presentation sends the message that you don't pay attention to detail, that you don't care about appearances, and that you don't respect your reader enough to be neat. So, here are a few general rules about presentation:

1. Proofread any letter before you send it out. And proofread it not just once, but twice—even three times.
2. Try to center your letter on the page to avoid having a large block of empty white space at the top or bottom.

3. Avoid excessive margins and don't crowd your writing to the edges of the page. In general, margins should be $1\frac{1}{2}$ inches all around.

PARTS OF A BUSINESS LETTER

Business letters can have up to 11 parts. You may not use all of them every time. They're listed below in the order in which they should appear in a letter.

WRITER'S ADDRESS

If your letter will not be sent on company letterhead, make sure your full name and address is the first item on your letter. Include your title and company name. This way your reader knows immediately who has sent them a letter. Write out all the words in this address (write *Street*, not *St.*) except the abbreviations for Mr., Mrs., Ms., Dr., and the state (*IN* instead of *Indiana*). Note: In business letters, the titles Mr., Mrs., and Ms., are often omitted in the writer's address. Dr., however, usually remains. Here's an example:

> Anthony Brown
> Union Delegate
> Regal Manufacturing
> 222 Chestnut Lane
> Cooperstown, OH 01101

DATE LINE

Next, type the month, day, and year. Write out the full name of the month (*September*, not *Sept.* or *9*) and use the number for the day (*12*, not *twelfth* or *12th*). Don't include the day of the week.

> April 3, 1997 (not Tues. 4/3/97)

INSIDE ADDRESS

Write the full name, title, company, and address of the reader. Don't abbreviate except for Mr., Ms., Mrs., and Dr. and the name of the state.

> Ms. Emily Warren
> Manager
> LMN Cleaners
> 557 Summit Avenue
> Whitehall, NY 10099

RE: OR SUBJECT LINE

Re: is an abbreviation for *regarding.* The *re:* line (often called the *subject line*) is a quick reference telling the reader what the letter is about. The *re:* line is not mandatory, but it's very helpful and it's almost always used in correspondence regarding legal matters or past due accounts. The *re:* line should be no more than a few words and is usually underlined. It can range from an account number to several words describing the letter's main subject:

> *Re:* Account # 4366

> *Re:* Revised Safety Standards

SALUTATION

The salutation is the greeting or opening of the letter. Begin with the word "Dear" and be sure your salutation properly reflects the formality of your relationship to the reader. Here are some guidelines for determining the proper salutation:

1. If you are not on a first-name basis with the reader, use Mr./Ms./Mrs. and the reader's last name (for example, *Dear Mr. Jones*).
2. If you don't know the reader's name, use Sir/Madam, or use the person's title (for example, *Dear Sir/Madam* or *Dear Customer Service Representative*).
3. If you know the reader's name but don't know whether the reader is male or female, do not assume or guess. Use Mr./Ms. ___ (for example, *Dear Mr./Ms. Jones*).

Follow the salutation with a colon (:).

BODY

The body of the letter (your actual message) is usually single spaced, with double spacing between paragraphs.

CLOSE

This is your "goodbye." There are several options for how to close your letter, and again, your close should reflect the formality of your relationship with your reader. The following list of closing words and phrases is ranked in order of formality, with 1 being the most formal:

1. Very truly yours,
2. Yours truly,
3. Sincerely yours,
4. Sincerely,
5. Cordially,
6. Best regards/best wishes,
7. Regards,
8. Best,
9. Yours,

Number 4, "Sincerely," is the most common close used in everyday business communications.

Only the first word of a close gets capitalized, and be sure to put a comma after the close.

Correct: Very truly yours,
Incorrect: Very Truly Yours

SIGNATURE

Four lines beneath your close, type your full name and, directly beneath that, your title. Sign your full name in the space between the two. However, if you are on a first-name basis with the reader, just your first name will do. Letters without signatures are generally not considered valid, and if someone else signs for you, it shows that you haven't taken the time to sign yourself.

STENO LINE/FILE NUMBER

If someone else types your letter for you—or if you are typing a letter for someone else—this should be indicated on your letter. One or two lines beneath your signature, the typist should write the initials of the letter sender in capitals followed by a slash (/) and then his or her own initials in lower case letters. Thus if you wrote the letter and your initials are JTE, and a typist with the initials DF typed it for you, the steno line would look like this:

JTE/df

If you type your own correspondence, there's absolutely no need for a steno line.

Sometimes, in combination with or in place of the steno line, there is a file name or number to indicate how the document has been saved, filed, or stored on the computer. Both conventions (the steno line and the file name or number) are used primarily to help track down documents and document errors.

ENCLOSURE

If you're enclosing documents with your letter, you need to include the enclosure line. Type "Enclosure" or "Enc." against the left-hand margin and then list the documents that are enclosed. For example:

Enclosures: Safety Guidelines
                  Employee Handbook

The enclosure line is used to clearly indicate what items have been sent along with the letter. If you don't enclose anything else with the letter, then you don't need to type the word enclosure on the letter.

CC/DISTRIBUTION

If people other than the addressee are to receive copies of your letter, and you want your reader to know that these people are receiving copies, then use the "CC" line. CC stands for carbon copy, a leftover from the days before copy machines when duplicates were made with carbon copy sheets. For example, if you were to write to someone and wanted to send a copy of that letter to your boss, you would double space down from the enclosure line and type the name of your boss:

CC: Jan Gallagher

If you want to copy several people, there are two choices for how to list those names: You can list these people in alphabetical order, or you can list them according to rank. You can also show their titles. In fact, if the addressee is not likely to know who these people are (or if they are likely to know each other), you should show their titles, as in the following example:

cc: Erik Lucas, President
Jennifer Alexander, Office Manager

Here, the cc's are ranked by title, not by alphabet. Generally, people who are mentioned in your letter or people who should know about the information in your letter should be copied. (Note: CC can be printed in the capital or lower case letters.)

COMMON BUSINESS LETTER FORMATS

These eleven parts of business letters are usually laid out on the page in one of two ways: block format or semi-block format. Both formats are discussed below.

BLOCK FORMAT

With the block format, each of the letter's 11 parts (including every paragraph in the body of the letter) is typed up against the left-hand margin. This is the simplest of the formats.

SEMI-BLOCK FORMAT

The semi-block format places most of the parts at the left-hand margin, but not all. The writer's address, date, close, and signature start at a tab in the middle of the page (the 4-inch mark, for example). Paragraphs in the body of the letter can be typed at the left-hand margin or they can be indented five spaces (this is often called the *modified* semi-block format).

On the next pages you will see the same letter printed in both block format and modified semi-block format.

Block Letter

Kisha Miller
Kruger Corporation
203 Elm Street
Smithtown, PA 19000

March 30, 1997

Customer Service Department
Ermine Parts Company
325 Baker Boulevard
Johnstown, PA 19009

Re: <u>Shipping error</u>

Dear Sir/Madam:

We recently ordered several replacement parts for our model 224 sorting machine. The shipment we received today had the right parts but for the wrong model. We are returning those parts to you by overnight mail. In the meantime, we have enclosed a copy of our original order and a copy of the packaging slip for the order we actually received.

We need these parts as soon as possible and would appreciate a prompt shipment of the correct parts.

Thank you.

Sincerely,

Kisha Miller

Enc: Copy of order
     Copy of packaging slip

CC: Charles Down, Facilities Manager

Modified Semi-Block Letter

Kisha Miller
Kruger Corporation
203 Elm Street
Smithtown, PA 19000

March 30, 1997

Customer Service Department
Ermine Parts Company
325 Baker Boulevard
Johnstown, PA 19009

Re: Shipping error

Dear Sir/Madam:

We recently ordered several replacement parts for our model 224 sorting machine. The shipment we received today had the right parts but for the wrong model. We are returning those parts to you by overnight mail. In the meantime, we have enclosed a copy of our original order and a copy of the packaging slip for the order we actually received.

We need these parts as soon as possible and would appreciate a prompt shipment of the correct parts.

Thank you.

Sincerely,

Kisha Miller

Enc: Copy of order
      Copy of packaging slip

CC: Charles Down, Facilities Manager

LETTERS OF TWO OR MORE PAGES

If your letter is more than one full page, the top of each additional page should include:

- The addressee's name
- The page number
- The date

This can be typed across the top of the page (all on one line) or on the first three lines of the page, at the left-hand margin, right-hand margin, or (if all on one line) centered. Here are two of those formats:

John Francis, Nov. 21, 1997, page 2. John Francis
                                        November 21, 1997
                                        Page 2

Many companies choose a certain style for their letters. Find out if your company prefers block or semi-block or has some other standard for letters. The more consistent a company is in how it presents itself to others, the greater the impression that the company cares about details and how it appears to the public.

PRACTICE

Take two letters from Chapters 6–11 and write or type them out in letter format. Make up the addresses to include. Use block format for one and semi-block for the other (with or without indented body paragraphs). Be sure to choose something that could be sent as a *letter* rather than a memo.

Possible Answers for Practice Exercises

The next page shows a sample letter in block format.

Robert Smith
ABC Corporation
123 Elm Street
Smithtown, PA 19000

March 30, 1997

Kisha Miller
Kruger Corporation
203 Elm Street
Smithtown, PA 19000

Dear Ms. Miller:

Thank you for requesting information about the workbench stools. We are proud of our wide selection and affordable pricing. Our most recent catalog is enclosed. Should you wish to order from us, you can expect to receive shipment within 2–4 weeks. Please let me know if you have any other questions or if I can be of further assistance. I look forward to your order.

Thank you.

Sincerely,

Robert Smith
Customer Service Representative

Enc: Catalog

IN SHORT

Letters that you write for work should have the standard business letter parts and fit into one of the standard business letter formats: block, semi-block, or modified semi-block format (unless your company has its own standard practices). Remember that neatness counts and if in doubt, put your comments in writing!

Skill Building Until Next Time

Look at the letters you receive at home from various businesses. Do they have all of the standard letter parts? In the right order? Do they use block, semi-block, or modified semi-block formats? You should notice that there is very little deviation from these formats.

CHAPTER | 13

Memos are used for most internal workplace communications. This chapter will show you the different parts of a memo and strategies for an easy-to-follow format.

MEMOS

External communications usually take the form of letters; internal communications, on the other hand, usually take the form of memos. A memo is the "letter" that is sent internally, within companies or organizations.

You may also have the occasion to write an external memo—a memo to someone outside of your company. It might be a company that you regularly communicate with for reasons not having to do with your normal money-making business. For example, if you and two other companies share a security service for your building and you had to communicate something regarding security, you'd send a memo instead of a letter.

The main difference between memos and letters is that memos are less formal. Like letters, they can have a variety of subjects, purposes, and formats, and all memos have the same parts. But because memos are less formal than letters, they only have half as many parts.

Memos are divided into six parts that fall into two main sections: the **heading** and the **body.** The heading shows who is writing to whom, when, and about what; the body then conveys the message.

Memo Notes

Memo is short for memorandum.

Memoranda is the plural form of memo.

HEADING

The heading of a memo should include the five parts listed below, in order.

To

List the recipients of the memo. Include first *and* last names *and* titles (or departments) for more formal memos or memos to superiors. Even if the subject is not formal, include titles if you're not sure everyone on the list knows everyone else on the list. If all recipients know each other's names and positions, then you can use just the first initial and last name of each recipient.

When you have several recipients, you have to decide how to list them. As with cc's on letters, you have two choices: list them alphabetically or by rank of position. Either order is acceptable.

If you are writing an external memo, then you should include the name of the company that each recipient works for as well.

If your memo is going to a lot of people, you don't have to list dozens of names. Instead, you can name the group or groups that the recipients belong to (so long as everyone in that group is getting the memo). Here are some examples:

TO: All Employees

TO: Production Managers
    Production Line Assistants

FROM

List the author(s) of the memo. You should generally list the name(s) and/or title(s) of the author(s) in the same way you've listed the name(s) and/or title(s) of the recipients. If the memo is from several people, follow the same rule: List them alphabetically or by rank.

DATE

List the month, date, and year just as you would in a letter (*March 28, 1997*, not *3/28/97* or *Mar. 28th '97*).

RE: OR SUBJECT LINE

The *re:* or subject line is much the same as the *re:* line in a letter, with one important exception: In a memo, the *re:* line should be more specific. It should still be short enough to fit on one line, but it should give readers a better idea of the subject matter of the memo. For example, compare the two *re:* lines below:

RE: Workman's Compensation

RE: Changes in Workman's Compensation Benefits for maintenance
    personnel

The first *re:* line is fine for a letter but too vague for a memo. The second *re:* line, however, tells readers a lot more and therefore is better for a memo. Why? Because at work, you generally deal with one business or one aspect of your company's business.

Someone in maintenance, for example, may get dozens of memos a week regarding repairs. If all the *re:* lines simply said "Repairs," he or she wouldn't be able to distinguish at a glance which memos were new request for repairs, repeat requests for repairs, reports about repairs, etc. Specific *re:* lines help personnel instantly prioritize their internal mail. Besides, these are your coworkers, so you should want to be as reader-friendly as possible. A specific *re:* line gives them the specific subject of your communication without forcing them to read your first few sentences.

DISTRIBUTION/CC

This part of a memo is just like the CC section of a letter. List those readers who are not direct recipients of your message but who should have a copy for their information or reference. The same rules apply for the order and format in which you list these names and/or titles.

BODY

The body of a memo is usually separated from the heading by a solid or dotted line or by several spaces. Some writers use asterisks (*) or other symbols. Check with your company to see if there's a routine way of separating the heading from the body.

The body of a memo, like the body of a letter, is usually single spaced with double spacing between paragraphs. Writers use several strategies to make the body of a memo easier to read and understand.

ORGANIZATION

First, the body of a memo is generally broken up into three parts that are roughly equivalent to an introduction, body, and conclusion. Thus, memos usually:

1. Start by stating the general facts, problem, or issue of discussion. What is the memo about? Begin with a clear topic sentence.
2. Then, state the facts or discuss the problem or issue. Provide support for the topic sentence.
3. Finally, discuss the significance of the facts, problem, or issue and/or request an action from your readers. In other words, what does this add up to? What should the reader do? See the example on the next page.

MEMORANDUM

TO: Group Leaders
FROM: Karen Hunt, Human Resources Manager
DATE: August 30, 1997
RE: Mandatory drug testing to begin for all employees
CC: Martin Lamb, Benefits Coordinator
           Christine Merlin, Vice President

Please inform all employees in your group that mandatory drug tests for all employees will begin on September 1. All employees will be required to take a urine test 4 times throughout the year and a blood test once every year. Urine tests will be unannounced, but the blood tests will be announced one day in advance. Employees found to have illegal substances in their blood or urine will be immediately suspended without pay and subject to investigation by the company.

It is important that employees understand the seriousness of this policy. Please distribute the attached announcement immediately.

If any employees in your group take controlled substances for medical purposes, they should contact Martin Lamb in Human Resources immediately.

Notice how the items in the heading are arranged and then notice how the information in the body is organized. The memo starts with a clear topic sentence, provides the specific facts, tells readers why this is important, and then calls for action.

READABILITY STRATEGIES

The memo on the previous page works well as a straightforward narrative, but many memos—especially long ones—are made much more readable by the use of the several "readability" strategies like the following. (Note: If you ever have the occasion to write a long letter, these same readability strategies apply.)

Headings

If the subject matter in your memo can be broken down into several sections, use headings to indicate those divisions. For example, if the drug testing memo were longer and more detailed, it might be broken down into the following sections with these headings:

- **Mandatory Drug Tests to Begin**
- **How Employees Will Be Tested**
- **Consequences of Testing Positive**

You could boldface, italicize, and/or underline these headings so it's clear that they're headings (but don't do all three). Headings are most clear if they are on a line by themselves, but as long as they are boldfaced, italicized, or underlined, they can begin a paragraph.

Lists

If your memo includes instructions or a number of items to be discussed, use lists. The items in your lists can be numbered, bulleted (•), or marked with letters of the alphabet. Here's one of the headings from the drug testing memo with a list added to it:

Consequences of Testing Positive

Employees who test positive will face the following consequences:

1. Employee will be immediately suspended without pay.
2. Employee must issue a statement explaining how he or she tested positive for illegal substances.
3. A three-member employee panel will be assigned to review the employee's case.

4. The panel will take into consideration the employee's statement and the employee's history with the company as well as the substance and amount for which the employee tested positive. Within one week of employee's suspension, the panel will make a recommendation regarding the employee.
5. Employee may appeal the panel's decision.
6. Employees are subject to review only after the first offense. On the second offense, employees will be terminated immediately and without review.

Bullets or letters could also have been used here in place of the numbers in the list. In any case, the text has been broken up so that it's easier to follow.

Tables and Graphs

If your memo includes a lot of numbers and statistics, use a table or graph to convey that information. For example, if you want to compare work-related accidents over the last three years, you could use a table like the following:

Year	Accidents
1994	15
1995	13
1996	11

This isn't exactly a lot of statistical information, but you get the idea. By putting information into a table or graph, you make it easier to read.

PRACTICE

Rewrite two exercises from Chapters 6–11 in memo format.

Possible Answer for Practice Exercise

MEMORANDUM

TO: Sharon Small, Assembler
FROM: Karen Hunt, Payroll Supervisor
DATE: July 29, 1997
RE: Recent errors in your paychecks
CC: Charles Good, Payroll Administrator

****

We deeply regret the recent error in your paychecks. We have discovered that there was an error in your account on the payroll system and we have corrected the problem. Your future checks should include the overtime pay you are due. We have also prepared a check for the overtime pay that is owed to you. You may pick up that check tomorrow morning.

IN SHORT

Memos are internal workplace communications that consist of a heading and body. The body of a memo has a three-part structure and often uses headings, lists, and tables or graphs to make its information more readable.

Skill Building Until Next Time

Look carefully at the next memos you receive at work. Notice how the headings are arranged and how the information in the body is organized. Do the memos use any readability strategies?

CHAPTER | 14

Reports are an important part of workplace writing and something you may need to write often. This chapter will show you the parts of a report and how these parts are formatted.

REPORTS

Company executives can't be everywhere at once, yet they need to know what's happening in every department in order to keep business running smoothly. They could never do this without reports.

As an employee you may be responsible for reporting to management on a number of issues: progress on projects, production, incidents, accidents, and so on. Here's a short list of some of the types of reports you may have to write:

- Meeting reports (minutes)
- Progress reports
- Periodic reports

- Trip reports
- Production reports
- Incident reports
- Accident reports
- Work reports

Some of these reports are written on a regular basis (every day, week, month, or year). Many of these reports will come to you pre-formatted; that is, the information you have to fill in will be clearly indicated and you will just have to fill in the blanks. For others, you'll have to start from scratch. Either way, you should know the general format for reports and some specific report formats.

REPORT FORMAT

Reports are generally designed to tell readers:

1. What you saw or heard
2. What you did
3. What you learned

Your report provides this information to a reader who will then make decisions or take actions based on your report.

HEADINGS OF A REPORT

Unlike letters or memos, most common workplace reports don't have many parts. They usually begin with a simple title that indicates their subject, like "Work Report" or "Accident Report," and then list the author and date of the report. Then, the body of reports usually follow a structure similar to the body of memos.

THE MAIN PORTION OF A REPORT

Most of a report—the body, so to speak—consists of an introduction, body, and conclusion.

Introduction

First, the beginning of a report introduces the subject and purpose of the report, often using a clear topic sentence like the following:

This is a report of work-related accidents from January 1, 1997, through June 30, 1997.

Reports may also begin with a sentence that summarizes the information to be contained in the report:

The number and type of work-related accidents for 1996 reflects an improvement in safety measures and standards.

If a report is to be filled out on a standard form, or if the report is one that employees fill out frequently, there's often no need for an introduction, because the information provided at the top of the form tells readers everything that would be in such a topic sentence. A sample report that does this appears later in this chapter.

Body

The paragraphs in the body of the report support the main idea. The more detailed and specific you are in this support, the better. Remember that the body of your report should not evaluate or assess the facts you report. Opinions or impressions should be reserved for the conclusion or recommendations section.

The body of a report, like the body of a memo, can be made reader-friendly by the use of headings, lists, tables, and graphs.

Conclusion

The conclusion should tell readers if there is any action to be taken or if there are any recommendations based upon what you've reported. For example, in a progress report, your conclusion might present your goals for the next report period or discuss problems you've been having during this report period. An accident report might recommend changes to be made to prevent similar accidents in the future.

Save Your Reader's Time

If your report is long or has a large amount of supporting data, you don't need to include all of that data in the report. Instead, summarize the data and include the full information or statistics as an attachment or appendix. For example, if you're reporting on all work-related accidents, you might summarize accident data and attach copies of all the accident reports.

TYPES OF REPORTS

Now let's look at how this report structure works for a few specific types of reports.

PROGRESS REPORT

Most reports follow a chronological order. A progress report, for example, will begin by naming the time period covered in the report. If it's a long and detailed report, it may also begin with a summary of what has been accomplished. Then the body will be organized as follows:

- Past: what has been accomplished
- Present: what work is in progress
- Future: future plans/goals and a time line for completion

Be specific about what you have accomplished and plan to accomplish. List any issues or concerns that you may have (things that may prevent you from achieving your goals, for example). Read the following progress report.

PROGRESS REPORT

For the week of: 11/13/96–11/20/96
Submitted by: Robert Evans
Department: Facilities

Completed:
- Repaired the damage to the roof from the weekend's ice storm. (This took two full days.)
- Replaced the pipes under the sink in the men's restroom.
- Repaired the cracks in the wall in the Conference Room.
- Replaced lightbulbs in the hallways.

In Progress:
- I have begun painting the cafeteria, but progress is slow because I am limited to the hours I can paint in there each day.

To Do (please rank in order of priority):
- Install the new window blinds that arrived yesterday.
- Clean up the branches and other debris from the ice storm.
- Continue painting the cafeteria. I had hoped to complete this task by the end of the week but since I have limited access to the cafeteria and am often interrupted when I'm in there, I may not finish until the end of next week.

LearningExpress

20 Academy Street, P.O. Box 7100, Norwalk, CT 06852-9879

To provide you with the best test prep, basic skills, and
career materials, we would appreciate your help.
Please answer the following questions and return this postage paid piece.
Thank you for your time!

Name : _____

Address : _____

_____

Age : _____   Sex : ☐ Male   ☐ Female

Highest Level of School Completed : ☐ High School ☐ College

1) I am currently :

    A student — Year/level: _____

    Employed — Job title: _____

    Other — Please explain: _____

2) Jobs/careers of interest to me are :

    1. _____

    2. _____

    3. _____

3) If you are a student, did your guidance/career counselor provide
you with job information/materials? _____

4) What newspapers and/or magazines do you subscribe to or
read regularly? _____

_____

5) Do you own a computer? _____

    If so, do you have Internet access? _____

    How often do you go on-line? _____

6) The last time you visited a bookstore, did you make a purchase?

_____

Have you purchased career-related materials from bookstores?

_____

7) Do you subscribe to cable TV? _____

    Which channels to you watch regularly (please give network
letters rather than channel numbers)?

_____

_____

8) Which radio stations do you listen to regularly (please give call
letters and city name)?

_____

_____

9) How did you hear about the book you just purchased from
LearningExpress?

    An ad? _____

    If so, where? _____

    An order form in the back of another book? _____

    A recommendation? _____

    A bookstore? _____

    Other? _____

10) Title of the book this card came from:

_____

LearningExpress books are also available in the test prep/study guide section of your local bookstore.

LEARNINGEXPRESS

The leading publisher of customized career and test preparation books!

LearningExpress is an affiliate of Random House, Inc.

Notice that there's no sentence naming the report period because the report form has a blank for that information. Notice also that the writer doesn't need transitions because of the way the report form divides the sections and because he has used bullets to list the items in his report. In addition, the writer mentions a concern about his ability to complete a certain project on time.

Most reports will follow this same basic structure.

INCIDENT REPORT

An incident report should be formatted as follows:

- Past: what happened
- Present: what the situation is now
- Future: what might happen or should happen (recommendations/concerns)

For your reference, see the reprint of the incident report from Chapter 6 on the next page.

TRIP REPORT

A trip report should be formatted as follows:

- Past: what you did or saw
- Present: how you feel about it, how you are using it in your work
- Future: how this can be used in your work, other trips, etc.

MEETING MINUTES

A report containing minutes for a meeting should be formatted as follows:

- Past: unfinished business from last meeting
- Present: current issues
- Future: when and where the next meeting will be held

Meeting minutes include the time and date of the meeting, who attended, and who would usually attend but was not there for this meeting.

INCIDENT REPORT

Submitted by: <u>Matthew Thomas</u>   Date of Incident: <u>1/21/97</u>
Position: <u>Security Guard, 2nd shift</u>   Time of Incident: <u>17 : 18</u>
Date of Report: <u>1/22/97</u>   Location of Incident: <u>Human</u>
                                                                    <u>Resources</u>

Description of Incident:
On Monday, January 22, at 16:32, Mr. R. Turner, a former employee, signed in at the security desk. He exchanged his driver's license for a visitor pass and put his destination down as Human Resources. At 17:18, I received a call from Maria Louis, the assistant director of Human Resources. She asked me to come to Human Resources immediately because Mr. Turner refused to leave the office and she could not lock up. I left Mark Davidson on duty at the desk and reached Human Resources at approximately 17:21. When I arrived, Mr. Turner was sitting by the receptionist's desk. I told Mr. Turner that the office was closed and that he had to leave. He said he would not leave until he saw John Francis, the director of Human Resources. Maria then told me that Mr. Francis was not in that day and that she told Mr. Turner several times that Mr. Francis was not in, but Mr. Turner did not believe her. She said Mr. Turner was waiting because he believed he would catch Mr. Francis as he tried to leave. Then I asked Mr. Turner if this was true, and he said yes. I told him that Mr. Francis was not in and that he could no longer sit in the Human Resources office. If he wished to wait, he could wait by the security desk, but he would be waiting until tomorrow morning. Then I asked Mr. Turner to follow me, and he did. After I escorted him to the security desk, I asked him if he wanted to wait or if he wanted his ID back. He said he'd come back later, so I returned his ID and he signed out at 17:30. Maria had followed us to the security desk, and after Mr. Turner left, she told me that Mr. Turner had just been fired for failing to pass a random drug test.

PRACTICE

1. Take the report you wrote in Chapter 6 and rewrite it in report form.
2. Write a progress report for your work in this book. You can follow the format of the sample listed in this chapter, but this report needs some kind of introduction.

Possible Answers for Practice Exercises

1. Answers will vary. Just make sure you follow the past, present, future format.

2. PROGRESS REPORT

Submitted by: Robert Evans

Date: 1/2/97

This a progress report for my studies in *Writing for Work*.

- I began with Chapter 1 last Monday. I have done one chapter each day and have now completed Chapters 1–13.
- I am currently working on Chapter 14, which I should finish today.
- I will complete this section (Chapter 15) this week and take the weekend off. Then I will complete the book by doing Chapters 16–20 next week.

Chapters 17 and 18 deal with clarity and style, which I think are my weaknesses, so I plan to pay particular attention to those chapters.

IN SHORT

Reports generally follow a three-part structure that begins with the subject of the report, provides the details of the report, and then concludes with comments or recommendations. Most common workplace reports are organized chronologically.

Skill Building Until Next Time

Your company probably has a variety of report forms for employees to fill out . If possible, get copies of some of those reports and samples of good reports. Look at how each type of report is arranged and see if you can determine what characteristics the good reports have in common.

CHAPTER | 15

When you want to propose a project or idea, you may need to write an official proposal. Proposals combine reporting with convincing. This chapter will show you how.

PROPOSALS

A proposal is a formal attempt to convince someone to approve, sponsor, agree to, or support a project or idea. Some examples of reasons to write proposals are:

- You have an idea that will cut your paperwork in half. How do you propose that idea?
- You want to take a few work-related courses at the local community college, but your company doesn't have an official tuition reimbursement policy. How do you propose that the company pay for your classes?

KINDS OF PROPOSALS

There are many different kinds of proposals, and they can range from the very complicated to the very simple. Generally, whatever the kind, proposals fall into one of three categories:

- Proposals to provide a good or service
- Proposals to make a change or improvement
- Proposals to approve a program or project

As an employee, you're most likely to encounter the second type, but the third type is common as well. And some proposals combine purposes. In any case, all proposals, complex or simple, follow this very basic organizational structure:

$$\text{problem} \rightarrow \text{solution}$$

Each of these types of proposals poses a problem and then offers a solution for it. Your job as a writer is to convince readers to accept or approve of the solution you offer.

Proposal Format
Discuss a problem and offer a solution.

PARTS OF A PROPOSAL

Proposals have several parts. Depending upon the length and complexity of the proposal, these parts may or may not be separated as individual sections, and not all parts are applicable for every proposal.

TITLE, AUTHOR, DATE, AUDIENCE

Make sure your proposal has a simple, direct title and that it indicates the date, the author of the proposal, and the receiver. For example:

Proposal to Reorganize Employee Report Forms
Submitted to: Alan Wilson
Submitted by: Lisa Green
Date: February 10, 1997

If you're writing your proposal in memo form, then this information will be taken care of in the heading of your memo, and you should not repeat it in the body.

PROBLEM STATEMENT

Describe the problem. Be sure to provide sufficient background information so that readers fully understand the problem.

DESCRIBE THE SOLUTION

First, use a general topic sentence to summarize the solution. Then provide the specific details of the solution. Readers need to know exactly what's involved in a solution before they can approve it. You can break the solution down into the following parts.

Procedures

If your solution requires several steps or complicated procedures, a procedures section will be helpful for readers. List the steps to be taken in chronological order. Readers need to know exactly what's involved in a solution before they can approve it.

Personnel

If several people will be working on this solution, explain who those people would be and why they'd be the best ones to accomplish those tasks.

Materials

If special equipment or materials are required for your solution, list that equipment or those materials.

Time Line

How long will this solution take? Can it be done in a day, a week, a year? Offer your best guess. You may want to provide a timeline as well.

Budget

How much will it cost to implement your solution? If there are large costs involved, it's a good idea to provide a budget—if you can offer accurate figures. Remember, when convincing, you need to anticipate readers' questions and objections, and one question they're sure to ask is "How much will this cost?"

Below is an example of a proposal for an idea that was discussed previously—creating a Spanish version of the employee training manual. This employee submitted her proposal on the company's proposal form.

GRAND IDEAS
Marlett Grand Hotel

Submitted by: Maritza Luz
Department/Title: Housekeeping Supervisor
Date: 8/21/97

Please describe your idea below.

As you know, over half of our employees speak Spanish as their native language, and many of them have not had a formal education in English. As a result, many of them have difficulty reading our Employee Training Manual, and I spend much of my time explaining things to employees that they should have learned from reading the manual.

I propose that we translate the manual into Spanish. If we had a version of the manual in their native language, these employees would complete training sooner and have a ready reference throughout their employment. In addition, I wouldn't have to spend as much time telling employees what they should already know.

I am fluent in both English and Spanish and have an excellent command of grammar in both languages. I would be happy to take on this project. I need only a few reference books costing a total of approximately $30, a computer to work on, and approval for overtime hours. I estimate that if I work an extra hour each day, I could have the manual translated in a month.

Notice that this proposal includes all of the parts except "procedures," which isn't really necessary here.

If this were a more extensive proposal with a lot of details for each part, you could use headers to separate the different parts and use lists and charts whenever possible.

Remember that the overall goal of a proposal is to convince. That means you need to:

- Show how your solution will clearly benefit readers
- Anticipate readers' reservations and objections
- Provide specific evidence for your claims

As you may recall, these points were covered in detail in Chapter 11, on the subject of "Convincing" your reader.

PRACTICE

Propose an improvement in how employees are treated or trained at your place of work, or propose a way to make something at work more cost effective, less time consuming, or otherwise more efficient and effective. Include all the parts of a proposal that are applicable.

Possible Answer to Practice Exercise

MEMORANDUM

TO: Bob Howard, Payroll Manager
FROM: Alexis Dern, Line Supervisor
DATE: August 4, 1997
RE: Proposal to revise time sheets

Wage-grade employees are currently required to fill out two different time sheets each week: one for regular hours and a separate form for overtime hours. This means that employees have to write their name, Social Security number, department, supervisor, and week begin/end dates on both sheets and get two supervisor signatures. This is a small but unnecessary waste of time which several employees in my group have complained about.

If the time sheets were combined so that regular and overtime hours can be reported on one form, this would no longer be a problem. Employees could fill out their personal information at the top, their regular hours in the middle, and any overtime hours at the bottom. A combined form would not only save some time each week but it would also save paper. All we need is for someone to design a new form, which should take just a few hours.

IN SHORT

Proposals use the problem-solution format to convince readers to accept a project or idea. They combine reporting and convincing skills to describe the problem and explain how the solution will be implemented. Your solution can be broken down into these parts: procedures, personnel, materials, timeline, and budget.

Skill Building Until Next Time

Companies that want your business will often send you letters that work like proposals: They address a problem or concern you may have and show how they could solve that problem. Look for such correspondence in the mail over the next couple of days and notice the different parts of the proposal at work.

SECTION | 4

TIPS FOR AN
EASY READ

The previous sections have shown you ways to develop, organize, and format your ideas. This section focuses on how to clearly and concisely express those ideas and make sure your writing is smooth and effective. In these five chapters, you'll learn:

- How to write effective introductions and conclusions
- How to write clearly
- How to write with an appropriate style
- How to revise
- How to edit

The chapters in this section aim to pull together all that you've learned so far, so that your communications are polished and effective.

CHAPTER | 16

Writers often get stuck
on introductions and
conclusions. This chapter
will give you strategies
and standard introductory
and concluding phrases
you can use to eliminate
writer's block for
these key areas.

INTRODUCTIONS AND CONCLUSIONS

For many writers, introductions and conclusions are the most difficult writing tasks. However, if you're armed with specific strategies for writing introductions and conclusions, you'll be able to all but eliminate this problem.

INTRODUCTIONS

The first piece of advice about introductions may surprise you. If you find yourself unable to write because you don't know how to get started, *skip the introduction*. Sometimes it's easier to get to the meat of what you're writing than to think of the perfect opening sentence. This doesn't mean you shouldn't have your purpose clearly in mind; it just means you should get something written and then come back to what kept you stuck.

However, even if you use this strategy, you still have to come back and write the introduction. This will be easier if you know exactly what belongs in an introduction and what introductions should do. In general, introductions should:

1. Tell readers what the communication is about (the subject).
2. Tell readers what you think, feel, or know about that subject (the main idea).

And sometimes introductions should:

3. Catch the reader's attention.

BEGIN WITH A CLEAR TOPIC SENTENCE

Numbers 1 and 2 should be obvious by now, so those will be discussed first. Although it's been mentioned it before, it bears repeating: When you're writing for work, one of the easiest and, in fact, one of the best ways to begin is to turn your purpose into a topic sentence. This means you have to do some brainstorming to clarify your purpose.

Here is a section reprinted from Chapter 3 to remind you of how to do this:

Topic:	new uniform policy
Audience:	all employees in production department
Purpose:	inform employees about the new uniform policy and when it begins
Topic sentence:	A new dress code for all employees will go into effect beginning on the first of the month.

Just about anything you write for work can use a topic sentence as its introduction. It's clear, straightforward, and right to the point.

USE STANDARD INTRODUCTORY PHRASES

Another option is to use standard introductory phrases. Most of these are actually variations of purpose statements, but because they've been used so often, they've become "standard." Here's a list of some of those standard introductory phrases. Feel free to use them, especially if you're stuck:

- It was a pleasure meeting/speaking with you . . .
- Thank you for . . .
- I am writing in response to . . .
- I am writing in regard to . . .
- I am writing to . . .
- As per your request . . .
- This is a reminder that . . .
- We are sorry to report/learn/hear . . .
- We are pleased to inform you . . .
- We regret to inform you . . .

Here are a few examples of complete introductory sentences that use these standard phrases:

As per your request, I have completed an inventory of all equipment and supplies in the shipping room.

I am writing to request that the broken oscillating fan in the shipping and receiving office be replaced as soon as possible.

Some proposals, letters, and memos require a different approach, and here's where purpose number 3 comes in. If your subject is something that may "get lost in the crowd," you may benefit from a catchy introduction. For example, remember Jennifer's memo trying to convince her coworkers to participate in the 5K run/walk for the Children's Hospital? Let's look at how she introduced that memo:

Time is money—and your time could mean money that's desperately needed for important medical research and services. I'm writing to ask for your time. As you may know, I volunteer at the Children's Hospital. Next month, the hospital is sponsoring a 5K run/walk. Will you participate? We need runners and walkers as well as volunteers to cover registration and t-shirt distribution. The run/walk is on Sunday, May 10, and starts at 9 a.m. If you'd like to participate, please call me at x3035. The registration deadline for participation is April 20. Please help us help children.

Notice how this introduction stands out because it's different from standard purpose-statement introductions. Catchy introductions can appeal to readers' needs, ask questions, use quotes, and anything else out of the ordinary. For example, here's another catchy introduction that could be used to begin this memo:

What if you could make a terminally ill child happy? What if you could help a sick child get better?

And another:

Run! Walk! Help! We need volunteers . . .

Catchy introductions can be very effective in getting your readers' attention, but they should be used only in appropriate situations. Informal writing to coworkers would be an appropriate situation, but an official memo to your supervisor would not. Most reports, for example, should not begin with this kind of introduction. It's best used in informal workplace writing.

PRACTICE A
Write a catchy introduction to a memo responding to Jennifer's request.

CONCLUSIONS
So you've finished the body of a letter, memo, or report. Now what? How do you end it? What makes a good conclusion?

When you're writing for work, a good conclusion is usually one that either *looks back* by returning to the topic sentence, or one that *looks ahead* to something the reader should do or something the writer expects.

CONCLUDING STRATEGIES

There are a number of ways you can look forward or back, and many of the examples below include standard concluding phrases. You'll see an example after each strategy to show you how it works.

1. Summarize or restate the main idea. This works best with longer texts.

   Once again, thank you for your help.

2. Make recommendations. This is a particularly useful conclusion for reports.

   Going forward, I think we should keep track of …

3. Look to the future. What do you look forward to doing or accomplishing?

   I look forward to working with you on this project.
   I hope to complete this inventory by Thursday.

4. Use a call to action. Tell your readers what they should do.

   Call Ximena by no later than Tuesday, August 1, if you will attend.
   Please respond by Friday, January 16.
   Fill out the attached form and return it as soon as possible.

5. Provide a reference person for readers to contact with questions or for more information.

   If you have any questions, please don't hesitate to call me at extension 333.
   Please call AnneMarie in Accounting for more information.

6. Thank your readers for their time or for what you're asking them to do.

   Thank you for your prompt attention to this matter.
   Thank you for your time.
   I appreciate your time and effort.

7. Remind readers why this matter is important to them.

   Remember, we cannot process your overtime sheets without a supervisor's signature.

PRACTICE B

Go back to three communications you've written for other exercises and write a different conclusion for each. Try to use three different strategies from the list above.

Possible Answers to Practice Exercises
Practice A

1. I am writing in response to your memo about the Children's Hospital 5K run/walk.
2. Okay! Okay! I will! I'd love to participate.

Practice B

These are three new conclusions for the memo regarding mandatory drug testing, from Chapter 13.

1. I appreciate your cooperation in distributing these announcements.
2. Mandatory drug testing may be a bit unsettling, but it is important for the health and safety of everyone here at RST Products.
3. We recommend that you hold a brief meeting with your group members to go over the policy carefully.

IN SHORT

Introductions and conclusions don't have to be a stumbling block. You can turn your purpose into an opening sentence or choose from several standard introductory and concluding phrases covered in this chapter.

Skill Building Until Next Time

Sales pitches that you receive in the mail often make use of catchy introductions and powerful conclusions. Other mail you receive will often rely on standard introductory and concluding phrases. Look for these approaches as you read your mail this week.

CHAPTER | 17

Effective writers never forget they're writing for a reader, and they make sure that all of their ideas come across clearly so there's no potential for confusion. This chapter focuses on practical ways you can write more clearly in all your workplace communications.

WRITING CLEARLY

In the work world, writing clearly and with an appropriate style means writing *without* gobbledygook. Take a look at the following example:

Dear Reader:

Because of the fact that this important chapter is of great significance, please hearken and take cognizance of the material that is herein presented within the pages included in this chapter.

Translation: *This chapter is important, so please pay attention.*

If only everything you read for work could be as clear and concise as this translation! Unfortunately, all too often it's not—and instead of clear, simple sentences like the one in this translation, you get confusing, roundabout, wordy, waste-of-my-time sentences like the one shown above the translation. In a word, gobbledygook.

To avoid being unclear in your writing, you must use an appropriate level of formality and get right down to business. In short, it means following these four rules:

1. **Be clear.**
2. **Be consise.**
3. **Use the right degree of formality.**
4. **Get straight to your point.**

This chapter covers rule 1. Rules 2–4 will be covered in the next chapter.

You must write clearly. If your reader can't understand what you've written, how can you achieve your purpose? You can't. Not only that, but you'll have mistreated your reader in the process, and that is one of the worst "crimes" a writer can commit. Read on for some strategies that writers use to help ensure their writing is clear to their readers.

AVOID JARGON

One of the most common flaws in workplace writing is the use of jargon. *Jargon* is technical or specialized language used by a limited audience. For example, you may know what an *adz* is, but unless your readers have had some experience with carpentry or woodwork, chances are *they* don't know. (It's a type of ax used for trimming or shaping wood.) Or you may know what the instructions "*Change to a sans serif font*" mean, but unless your readers have had experience in word processing or typesetting, they probably won't. (A sans serif font is a type style and size that doesn't have small lines finishing off the strokes in the letters. This is a <u>serif</u> font; this is a <u>sans serif</u> font.)

> **Writing with Clarity**
> Clarity is the quality of being clear.

The key to avoiding jargon, then, is to be sure that you write at the appropriate level for your readers. This is why it's so important to know who your readers are. Will they understand you if you use technical language? If you're an electrician and you're writing to other electricians, sure. But if you're an electrician and you're writing to someone in accounting, for example, you'll confuse your reader if you use electrician jargon.

If you must use jargon and your audience is not technical or won't be familiar with your specialized terms, then be sure to *define those terms* for your readers as in the following example:

> Before painting the mullions (the wooden or metal bars between the panes of the window), it's a good idea to line the edges of the panes with tape.

This is also true of abbreviations. If you use an abbreviation readers may not know, be sure to define it:

> The wages on the PS (Postal Service) Schedule are different from the wages on the MH (Mail Handler) Schedule.

PRACTICE A

Are the following passages from the chapter entitled "Wage Grade Occupations in Federal Service" in the book *Working for Your Uncle: The Complete Guide to Finding a Job With the Federal Government* (Ossining, NY: Breakthrough Publications, 1993) too technical for a general (non-technical, non-specialized) audience? Answers to all practice exercises are at the end of the chapter.

1. **Coin/Currency Checking**
   This occupation includes jobs involved in visually examining (1) finished coins and medals for finish, appearance, discoloration, missing letters, etc., or (2) U.S. currency, stamps, bonds, and other paper security documents to detect imperfections.

2. **Toolmaking**
   This occupation includes jobs involved in the fabrication, manufacture, calibration, reconditioning, and repair of machine tools, jigs, fixtures, dies, punches, and gauges used in the manufacture, overhaul, and repair of equipment.

AVOID PRETENTIOUS LANGUAGE

Pompous or *pretentious language* is another matter. This is a common error because inexperienced writers often believe that big words impress readers. Listen carefully: They don't. It's *clear writing* that impresses readers. Sometimes a big, multi-syllable word is the one that most clearly expresses the idea you want to convey, and that's fine. But there's no need for a sentence like the following:

Pretentious:	I arose to a bipedal position and perambulated the circumference of the quadragonal enclosure.
Plain English:	I stood up and walked around the room.

Similarly, there's no need to use words like *utilize* or *facilitate—use* and *help* are just fine, and often clearer. You don't add any authority or value to what you write by using big words when short, simple, clear words will do.

Remember that clarity comes first, and simple, clear words at the right level of technicality for your reader will keep you on that track.

PRACTICE B

Rewrite the following sentences to eliminate pretentious language. (Use a dictionary to look up unfamiliar words.)

1. The remuneration you've apportioned me is incommensurate with my dextrousness and experience with the erection of edifices.
2. That homo sapiens of the male gender is devoid of monetary resources.

AVOID AMBIGUOUS LANGUAGE

Ambiguous means *having two or more possible meanings*. So of course ambiguous words and phrases also interfere with clarity. Take a look at this sentence, for example:

The photographer shot the model.

Notice that this sentence can be read two ways: Photographers "shoot" pictures with a camera, but this sentence can also mean that the photographer shot the model with a gun, not with a camera. This kind of ambiguity happens whenever a word has more than one possible meaning by the way it's used in a sentence. The ambiguous sentence above should be revised to read:

The photographer *took pictures of* the model.

"Took pictures" isn't as powerful a verb as "shot," but at least there's no ambiguity, and no need to call the police.

Another type of ambiguity happens when a series of words is in the wrong place in a sentence. For example, look at the following sentence:

The woman ate the sandwich with a blue hat.

Here, the *word order* of the sentence, not an individual word, causes the confusion. Did the woman eat her sandwich with her hat? That's what the sentence actually says, but of course that's not what the writer intended. Because the phrase *with a blue hat* is in the wrong place, the sentence becomes unclear. This sentence should be revised to read:

The woman *with a blue hat* ate a sandwich.

Here's another ambiguous sentence:

When reaching for the phone, the coffee spilled on the table.

The sentence, as written, means that *the coffee* reached for the phone. Therefore, the word order needs to be rearranged. A missing word also needs to be added—the subject of the sentence—to fully eliminate the ambiguity:

The coffee spilled on the table when *he* reached for the phone.
He spilled the coffee on the table when reaching for the phone.

PRACTICE C

Eliminate any ambiguity in the following sentences.

1. When writing on the computer, the spell checker often comes in handy.
2. The famous artist drew stares when he entered the room.
3. I went to see the doctor with a severe headache.

AVOID UNCLEAR PRONOUN REFERENCES

A third item that interferes with clarity is unclear pronoun references. (Pronouns, remember, are words like *me, you, he, she,* and so on that replace nouns.) Here's an example of an unclear pronoun reference:

I went to the meeting with Ted and Fred, and we took his car.

Whose car? "His" could mean either Ted's or Fred's. Perhaps only Fred has a car, so the writer thought there was no need to explain that it was Fred's car. But remember that your reader may not know what you know, and it's dangerous to assume otherwise. In fact, it's best *never* to *assume* your reader knows background information that you know. This way you won't make the mistake of leaving out information your reader may need.

Here's another example of an unclear pronoun reference:

It's been years since they tore down that building.

This is an example of a common pronoun error: using a vague "they" when there are specific people behind an action, but you don't know exactly who those people are. Still, you know enough to say something like:

It's been years since *a demolition crew* tore down that building.

Here's another example of a vague "they":

Vague:	*They* passed a new tax law yesterday.
Clear:	*The State Senate* passed a new tax law yesterday.

Be careful of this vague "they." There are always people behind their actions, and your sentences should say so.

PRACTICE D

Eliminate unclear pronoun references from the following sentences.

1. Mr. Jones told Mr. James that he had found his missing report.
2. They closed the movie theater after they discovered several fire code violations.
3. The police officer arrested the man after he attacked a sales clerk.

USE THE ACTIVE VOICE WHEN POSSIBLE

Using the active voice means making sure a sentence has a clear agent of action and a direct approach. For example, compare the following sentences:

Passive:	The file was put in the wrong drawer.
Active:	Someone put the file in the wrong drawer.

Notice how the active sentence gives readers an agent of action—a subject performing a verb. In the passive sentence, you don't know who or what put the file in the wrong drawer; you just know that somehow it got there. The active sentence doesn't give readers a name, but it does give them an agent of action and as a result a more direct sentence. It can also often help to reduce the number of words needed to express an idea:

Passive:	The file *was put* in the wrong drawer *by somebody.* (10 words)
Active:	*Somebody put* the file in the wrong drawer. (8 words)

The active voice also makes a sentence sound more authoritative and powerful—*someone* is doing *something*. In a passive sentence, someone or something has something done to it.

However, there are times when the passive voice makes sense—like when you don't know the agent of action or when you want to emphasize the action, not the agent. It's also useful when you desire anonymity or objectivity. For example:

- *The location was deemed suitable by the committee.* (Here, the passive voice emphasizes the action of the committee rather than the committee).
- *He was fired.* (The passive voice provides anonymity by not giving an agent of action. Thus, no one has to take the blame for firing him.)

PRACTICE E

Make the following sentences more direct by turning the passive voice into the active.

1. Protective gear must be worn by all employees when entering the honeycomb area.

2. The new policy was described by Ms. Wynn at the meeting.

3. Four months of on-the-job training were completed by me.

Possible Answers to Practice Exercises

Practice A
1. This is probably not too technical.
2. This is too technical because the words are too difficult for general readers to understand.

Practice B
1. The salary you offer is not equal to my construction skills and experience.
2. That man is broke.

Practice C

1. When you write on the computer, the spell checker often comes in handy.
2. The famous artist was stared at when he entered the room. Or: People stared at the famous artist when he entered the room.
3. I went to see the doctor about my severe headache.

Practice D

1. Mr. Jones told Mr. James that he had found James' missing report.
2. The fire inspector closed the movie theater down after a local citizen discovered several fire code violations.
3. The police officer arrested the man who had attacked a sales clerk.

Practice E

1. All employees must wear protective gear when entering the honeycomb area.
2. Ms. Wynn described the new policy at the meeting.
3. I completed four months of on-the-job training.

IN SHORT

You need to write clearly in workplace writing. Avoid jargon, pretentious language, ambiguity, and unclear pronoun references, and make sure most sentences have a direct agent of action.

Skill Building Until Next Time

Watch for examples of jargon, pretentious language, ambiguity, and unclear pronoun references and the passive voice in the things you read this week.

CHAPTER | 18

This chapter focuses on workplace writing style. Specifically, the three rules of writing clearly are covered: being concise, using the appropriate level of formality, and getting straight to the point.

WRITING WITH STYLE

Clarity is essential, but clarity alone does not make good workplace writing style. Also important are these three rules for workplace writing, which should look familiar to you because you saw them in the previous chapter:

1. Be concise.

2. Use the right degree of formality.

3. Get straight to your point.

BE CONCISE

Time is money, and in workplace writing, you can't afford to waste your reader's time by taking too long to convey your message. Readers are quickly annoyed by writers who take ten sentences to say what could be expressed in four or five. Being an effective writer at work means being very attentive to the need for being concise. Below are some ways to avoid wordiness and write concisely.

AVOID CLUTTER

Here is a list of several words, phrases, and constructions that add clutter to your writing.

1. **Because of the fact that.** In most cases, just "because" will do.

   Because of the fact that it rained, the game was canceled.
   Because it rained, the game was canceled.

2. ***That* and *which* phrases** often clutter needlessly and can usually be rephrased. Simply turn the idea in the *that* or *which* phrase into an adjective.
   This is a manual *that is very helpful.*
   Thus is a very *helpful* manual.

   The meeting *which lasted five hours* ended at four.
   The *five-hour* meeting ended at four.

3. **There is, it is.** Remember the direct approach? The *there is* and *it is* constructions avoid the direct approach and use unnecessary words in the process. Instead, use a clear agent of action.

   It is with regret that we must decline your kind offer.
   We regret that we must decline your kind offer.

   There is no reason we can find to disagree.
   We can find no reason to disagree.

   The revised versions are not only two words shorter—they're also more direct.

4. That by itself is a word that often clutters sentences unnecessarily.

> He said that he thought ~~that~~ the meeting was useful and that he was happy ~~that~~ there will be a follow-up meeting.

You could do away with all of the *thats* in this sentence, but if you want to keep a couple, they should be the one before "he thought" and the one before "he was happy" to help the reader understand the passage.

PRACTICE A

Revise the following sentences to eliminate clutter words, phrases, and constructions. Answers to all practice exercises are at the end of the chapter.

1. The employees who were late missed the first set of awards.

2. It is my feeling that we should hire her immediately.

3. I believe that there is the possibility that the manager who was recently hired is not too fond of me.

AVOID UNNECESSARY REPETITION

When writers are not sure that they've been clear, or when they are simply not being attentive to their reader's need for concise writing, they often repeat themselves unnecessarily by saying the same in two different ways. This is what happened in the following example:

Wordy: We will meet at 4 p.m. in the afternoon.
Concise: We will meet at 4 p.m.

The abbreviation "p.m." *means* in the afternoon, so there's no reason to say "in the afternoon." It's a waste of words and of the reader's time.

Here are some more examples:

Wordy: The room is red in color.
Concise: The room is red.

Wordy: It is essential that everyone arrive promptly and on time.
Concise: It is essential that everyone arrive on time.

PRACTICE B

Eliminate unnecessary repetition in the following sentences.

1. It's time to terminate the project and put an end to it.
2. The car that is grey in color must have been in an accident or collision.
3. Please let me know your plans as soon as possible and at your earliest convenience.

USE EXACT WORDS AND PHRASES

A lot of wordiness can often be trimmed by using *exact* words and phrases. This means substituting a strong, specific word for a weak, modified word or phrase. (A modifier is a word that describes, like *red* balloon or *very juicy* apple.) Notice how exactness cuts back on wordiness and makes for much more powerful sentences in the following examples:

He *walked very forcefully* into the room.
He **burst** into the room.

I *am not in agreement*.
I **disagree**.

Please *give consideration* to our proposal.
Please **consider** our proposal.

He *is of the opinion that* this project will be a success.
He **believes** this project will be a success.

She was *very upset* by the news.
She was **devastated** by the news.

PRACTICE C

Revise the following sentences to make them more exact.

1. We are of the understanding that the deal is off.

2. He looked at the problem very carefully.

3. She is planning to say yes to the job offer.

USE THE PROPER LEVEL OF FORMALITY

Whenever you write, you must decide on a level of formality that ranges from very formal (proper, stuffy, distanced) to very informal (slangy, relaxed, intimate). In most cases, you should fall somewhere near the middle of the scale but on the formal side.

As the person you write to increases in rank, so should your level of formality. The less familiar a person is to you, the greater your level of formality. Look at the following scale:

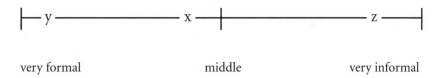

very formal   middle   very informal

When writing to your superior, even if you are friends, you should fall just to the left of the middle, around the "x". If, on the other hand, you write to the president of the United States, you might want to be somewhere near the "y" at the top of the scale. Similarly, in a letter to a close friend, your level of formality will probably be close to "z" at the other end of the scale.

How exactly does this translate for you as a writer? It mostly boils down to word choice.

You could say: We would like to *get* a new computer.

Or you could say: We would like to *buy* a new computer.

Or: We would like to *purchase* a new computer.

Get, buy, and *purchase* all mean essentially the same thing here, but they vary in degree of formality, with *get* being the least formal and *purchase* being the most formal. Thus, once you've established where you should fall on the formality scale, you need to choose your words accordingly.

PRACTICE D

Rank the following words in order of formality, with 1 being the least formal and 3 being the most formal:

__ permit
__ let
__ allow

__ remove
__ eliminate
__ get rid of

__ crash
__ collision
__ accident

GET RIGHT TO THE POINT

To say it once more: Time is money, so not only should you not waste your readers' time with wordiness, you should also not waste your reader's time with small talk. When you write for work, get right to the point. If the person you are writing to for work is also a close friend, talking about personal life may be okay, but in most cases, even friendly small talk is inappropriate. The memo below provides an example.

TO: Jennifer West
FROM: Brenda East
DATE: February 11, 1997
RE: Purchase order for new computer monitor

_____

How are you? I saw the picture that your son drew for you hanging in your office. It's wonderful! He'll be a great artist some day.

Anyway, I'm writing to ask about the purchase order I recently submitted for a new monitor…

First of all, you should probably *tell* Jennifer what you think of her son's drawing if you feel strongly enough to want to write about it. After all, a personal message is best delivered in person. Second, the first paragraph here has nothing to do with the matter at hand. If you wish to get personal or add a friendly comment or two, do it at the end of your letter or memo—in no case should there be a personal message in a report or proposal—*after* you've taken care of business. You show more respect for your reader by getting straight to the point than by starting off with small talk.

Possible Answers to Practice Exercises
Practice A
1. The late employees missed the first set of awards.
2. I feel we should hire her immediately.
3. I believe the new manager may not be too fond of me.

Practice B
1. It's time to terminate this project.
2. The grey car must have been in an accident.
3. Please respond as soon as possible.

Practice C
1. We understand that the deal is off.
2. He studied the problem. Or: He scrutinized the problem.
3. She plans to accept the job offer.

Practice D
3. permit
1. let
2. allow

2. remove
3. eliminate
1. get rid of

1. crash
3. collision
2. accident

IN SHORT

When writing for work, it's important to follow these rules of style: Be clear, be concise, use the right level of formality, and get right to the point.

Skill Building Until Next Time

Journalists are experts in writing clearly and concisely. Review some newspaper articles to see these writing strategies at work.

CHAPTER | 19

Even the best writers
don't get it right
the first time. This
chapter will teach you
specific strategies for
the all-important
task of revising, or
rewriting what
you've written.

REVISING
STRATEGIES AND
CHECKLISTS

Back in the introduction to this book, you
read a statement that may have surprised you: writing *is* revising.
The process of revision means just that: ***re-vision***, to look at
again. In other words, revising means reviewing what you've written to
make sure that:

1. It does what it's supposed to do
2. It does it effectively

If it doesn't, or if it can be done better, you need to rewrite it.

You've already done some revising in various exercises throughout
the book, especially in the previous two chapters on writing clearly and

style. This chapter is about "big picture" revising: revising for larger concerns like content (ideas and information) and organization. Revising for style, grammar, and format are discussed in the next chapter.

TWO HELPFUL HINTS FOR REVISING

Before you begin to look at specific "big picture" revising concerns, keep the following two hints for revising in mind.

GET FEEDBACK

First, don't forget the techniques mentioned in the introduction for *getting feedback:* reading aloud and showing your work to someone else. Reading your work aloud enables you to hear how your writing sounds and catch confusing ideas and errors. By showing your work to others, you can get objective feedback about how well you've fulfilled your purpose.

GIVE YOURSELF TIME TO REVISE

Don't expect to write and revise a perfect memo or proposal in ten minutes. In fact, the earlier you begin your writing task, the better, because a little distance always helps. That is, if you draft your communication and then sit down to revise it right away, your draft may be too fresh in your head for you to think clearly about revisions. However, if you can put what you've written aside for a while—even if it's just for 15 minutes while you have a cup of coffee—when you come back, you will be able to think more clearly and creatively about what you've written.

REVISING STRATEGIES

Now to some specific revising strategies. Here is a checklist of things to look for when revising. Follow it in the order listed because it starts with the most global issue and moves down to more specific concerns. Here's the checklist in a nutshell:

_____ clear purpose
_____ sufficient support
_____ logical organization
_____ readability factor
_____ strong transitions
_____ effective and appropriate introduction
_____ effective and appropriate conclusion

CHECK FOR A CLEAR PURPOSE

Remember that your purpose is what drives your communication, and your purpose should be made clear for your reader from the very beginning. You should look specifically for three things:

_____ Is your main idea expressed in a clear topic sentence?

_____ Is your main idea general enough to cover everything that you discuss in your communication?

_____ Is your main idea expressed in one of the first sentences, if not the first?

If you answer "no" to any of these questions, go back and revise. For a review of how to clearly express your purpose in your main idea, see Chapter 3.

CHECK FOR SUFFICIENT SUPPORT

Once your main idea passes the revising test, check that you've provided sufficient support for that main idea. Remember that support can come from many sources, including:

_____ details

_____ reasons

_____ examples

_____ results

_____ definitions

_____ comparisons

_____ quotations or expert opinion

_____ statistics

_____ descriptions

_____ anecdotes

Whether your main idea is a matter of fact or a matter of opinion, you need supporting ideas to give your main idea credibility. Especially if you are trying to convince, the more support, the better.

You should also make sure that your support is the kind that you need to adequately fulfill your purpose. For example, if your purpose is to convince, have you shown your readers how they would benefit from agreeing to what you ask? Have you considered readers' reservations and objections? If your purpose is to complain, have you made it clear exactly what's wrong with the product, service, or item you're complaining about?

For a general review of how to provide strong support, see Chapter 4. For how to support different purposes, see the appropriate chapter in Section 2.

CHECK FOR LOGICAL ORGANIZATION

As you know by now, there are many organizing principles writers can use to arrange their ideas logically. Writers organize ideas:

____ chronologically
____ by cause and effect
____ spatially
____ by analysis/classification
____ by order of importance
____ by comparison and contrast
____ by problem and solution

If you read what you've written and the ideas seem out of order, or if it seems as if your communication jumps around, you should take a look at your organizing principle. Is there one? Have you used it properly? For a review of organizing principles, see Chapter 5.

CHECK FOR THE READABILITY FACTOR

Good writers have one rule that they never break: *Always respect the reader.* This means, in part, making sure their ideas are as easy for readers to follow as possible. One way to do this is to organize information in clear chunks of related ideas. Writers do this naturally by separating sentences into paragraphs. But sometimes writing in nothing but paragraphs, especially when there is a list of several items, isn't the most "readable" format for presenting the information. Readability can be enhanced by the use of:

_____ *Headings:* Create brief "titles" indicating the general subject of each section.

_____ *Lists:* Use bullets, numbers, or letters of the alphabet to separate the items in your list.

_____ *Tables and graphs:* Organize your information visually.

As a general rule, if you have more than three items of information on one topic, you should consider using one of the readability strategies above. For examples, choose any chapter in this book and look at how these three strategies help organize information to make it more readable.

CHECK FOR STRONG TRANSITIONS

Just as a train needs physical links between each railway car, when you write, your ideas need to be held together by transitions to effectively show the relationship between your ideas. When you write without transitions, it's like asking your readers to jump from stone to stone across water because you haven't bothered to build them a bridge. So, check for strong transitions. Here are a few transitional words and phrases to jog your memory:

_____ however

_____ next

_____ then

_____ since

_____ while

_____ on the other hand

_____ likewise

_____ for example

A good way to check for strong transitions is to reread what you've written and circle all of the transitional words and phrases you can find. There should be several words that come from the list in Chapter 5 as well as others that are appropriate to the context of your message. If you seem to have very few words circled, you should probably check your writing again to see if connections between ideas could be stronger. For a review of transitions, see Chapter 5.

CHECK FOR AN EFFECTIVE AND APPROPRIATE INTRODUCTION

As much as you might wish otherwise, first impressions count, and how you introduce ourselves to others can determine how others perceive (and receive) you. The same is true of writing. How you introduce your ideas can make a big difference in how your ideas are received.

When you're writing for work, the most common, practical, and sensible introduction is to begin with a clear topic sentence that states your purpose. That is, your opening sentences should:

- Tell readers the subject of your communication
- Tell readers the general idea that you want to convey about that subject (what you think, feel, or know about that subject)

There are two ways you can accomplish this. The first and often the easiest method is to simply turn your purpose statement into a topic sentence (see "Check for a clear purpose" above). The second method is to rely, if possible, on a standard introductory phrase, like "I am writing in response to" or "As you requested."

If what you're writing is less serious or formal in nature and if it is something that you don't want to be overlooked, you can try a catchy introduction. Because so much of writing for work uses the types of introductions just mentioned, catchy introductions will really stand out. Catchy introductions, though, are most appropriate for informal workplace situations. Be sure to use your judgment. For a review of introductions, see Chapter 16.

CHECK FOR AN EFFECTIVE AND APPROPRIATE CONCLUSION

Appropriately, the last item on the checklist is conclusions. How should you end a workplace communication? There are many specific strategies, but they all break down into two categories of conclusions:

- Conclusions that look back at what has been said or done
- Conclusions that look ahead to what will be done or what the writer expects

Specifically, you could conclude by:

_____ summarizing or restating the main idea

_____ making recommendations

_____ stating what you're looking forward to

_____ asking or telling reader(s) to take a specific action

_____ providing a reference person for questions or future action

_____ thanking readers

_____ reminding readers why the matter is important to them

By looking ahead or looking back, you'll give readers a feeling of closure (that you've said all you have to say about the subject) and a feeling that your communication has amounted to something worthwhile for them. Thus, the stronger your concluding sentence(s), the better. For more review of conclusions, see Chapter 16.

PRACTICE

The following is a rough draft of a memo. Keeping in mind the purpose below, revise this memo using the strategies discussed in this chapter. You should be able to use all seven revising strategies.

Purpose: to point out a problem with theft from employees and suggest ways to prevent future crimes

There has been a lot of theft in our building recently. Yesterday I was a victim. It happened in the employee locker room. There are several ways we could reduce theft in the building. We could use combination locks instead of keys for lockers. Install cameras in key locations throughout the building. Hire more security officers. Hire an undercover employee. My watch and $10 were stolen from my jacket pocket. The locker room is the most common site of these thefts.

Possible Answer to Practice Exercise

This memo needs help in all seven areas:

1. It lacks a clear topic sentence explaining the writer's purpose.
2. It lacks sufficient support for its assertion that "there is too much crime in our building." We need to hear other examples of recent thefts. And the more detailed and specific, the better. How many thefts? Of what nature?

3. The information is not organized logically; the reader must jump from the problem to possible solutions and back to the problem again, and the problem—the specific incident—is not told in chronological order. (Notice there's a clear topic sentence introducing the problem and a second clear topic sentence introducing possible solutions.)

4. The possible solutions are perfect candidates for a list to make them more readable.

5. There are few, if any, transitions between sentences in this paragraph.

6. This memo needs a clear purpose-centered introduction. It could also begin with a catchy introduction, since it's an important but not formal subject and since it doesn't have to do with increasing the bottom line and therefore may get lost in the crowd.

7. It also needs a conclusion that looks ahead or looks back. It would be appropriate for this memo to look ahead and call for action

Here is one way this memo could be revised:

I'm writing to call your attention to a very disturbing fact. In the last three months, there have been over a dozen incidents of theft on company property. Yesterday, I was the latest victim. My watch and $10 were stolen from my jacket pocket. My jacket was in the employee locker room, which is the most common site of these thefts. Last week, for example, Shannon Weil's purse was stolen from the employee locker room. Two weeks before that, Roger Blackman had bought a present for his wife during his lunch hour and it, too, was stolen from the locker room. In addition, thefts have occurred in the lunchroom (employee lunches and thermoses) and in work areas. Arnold Proust, for example, had his calculator and $5 stolen from his desk drawer.

There are several simple measures we could take to reduce theft in the building. For example, we could:
- Use combination locks instead of keys for lockers.
- Install cameras in key locations throughout the building.
- Hire more security officers.
- Hire an undercover employee.

Clearly we have a security problem that must be addressed. Please consider implementing one or more of these security measures so that I will be the latest and the *last* victim.

IN SHORT

When you revise, begin with the "big picture" concerns: a clear purpose; strong, detailed support; logical organization; readability; strong transitions; and effective introductions and conclusions.

Skill Building Until Next Time

Keeping this checklist in mind, are there things you've written recently that need revising? In what areas do they need the most work? If you notice a pattern (for example, several of your messages seem to lack sufficient support), you may want to review the corresponding chapter.

CHAPTER | 20

In addition to revising for content, writers need to revise for style and to edit their documents for correct grammar, mechanics, and format. This chapter will show you what to look for and how to correct your mistakes.

EDITING STRATEGIES AND CHECKLISTS

Once you've revised for the "big picture," it's time to put away your telescope and take out your microscope. Rather than looking at your text as a whole, you now have to look at its individual parts—sentences—and check for proper workplace writing style. Are your ideas expressed in clear, concise sentences at the appropriate level of formality? Do you get right to the point?

In addition, you need to edit what you've written. Revising deals with ideas; editing deals with grammar (correct sentences), mechanics (correct capitalization, spelling, and punctuation), and format (correct arrangement on the page).

Here's an outline of sentence-level revising and editing concerns:

Revising vs. Editing

Revising focuses on the "big picture" of your overall purpose and ideas. Editing focuses on particular details, such as grammar, mechanics, and format.

Check for appropriate style:

_____ Are your sentences clear?

_____ Are your sentences concise?

_____ Have you used the appropriate level of formality?

_____ Does your communication get right to the point?

Check for grammar:

_____ Are all sentences complete?

_____ Have you checked for run-on sentences?

_____ Are your verbs in the proper tense?

Check for mechanics:

_____ Are the proper items capitalized?

_____ Are sentences properly punctuated?

_____ Are all words spelled correctly? Have you checked for typing errors?

Check for format:

_____ Does your document have proper margins? Is it relatively centered on the page?

_____ Does your document have all of the parts it should have and in the order in which it should have them?

_____ Is your document printed neatly?

CHECK FOR APPROPRIATE STYLE

Style is *how* you say what you say—the words you choose and how you organize those words in sentences. As you recall, there are four rules for workplace writing style. You should check that you've followed each of these rules before you send out your communication.

ARE YOUR SENTENCES CLEAR?

_____ Check for jargon and pretentious language. Unless you're writing for a specialized audience, eliminate any jargon, and no matter who your audience, get rid of any pretentious language you find.

_____ Check for ambiguity. Are there any words that can have more than one meaning in the context of the sentence? Are there any sentences where the word order might confuse readers?

_____ Check for unclear pronoun references. Are there any pronouns that could refer to more than one person or thing mentioned in the sentence? Are there any vague *they*s that need to be clarified?

_____ Check for active sentences. Make sure your sentences have a clear agent of action, unless you want to emphasize the action of the sentence or unless you desire anonymity.

ARE YOUR SENTENCES CONCISE?

_____ Check for clutter words, phrases and constructions like *because of the fact that*, *that* and *which* phrases, and *there is* and *it is* constructions.

_____ Check for unnecessary repetition.

_____ Check for exact words and phrases. Do you have weak, modified words or phrases that could be replaced by strong, specific words?

HAVE YOU USED THE APPROPRIATE LEVEL OF FORMALITY?

_____ Remember the formality scale. Considering your audience, are you on the right place on that scale? Do your word choices match where you should be on that scale?

DO YOU GET RIGHT TO THE POINT?

_____ Remember that workplace writing style avoids small talk. Show respect for your reader by getting right to the point.

CHECK FOR GRAMMAR

Grammar is the rules that govern sentences. This is not a grammar book so its purpose is not to review all of the rules you've learned over the years in school. But you should be aware of a few areas where writers most often make grammatical mistakes.

COMPLETE SENTENCES

Remember that each sentence must have a subject (who or what performs the action) and a verb (an action) in order to be complete.

Incomplete: When it rains.
Complete: When it rains, the roof leaks.

Incomplete: After I put the file back in the proper drawer.
Complete: Afterwards, I put the file back in the proper drawer.

RUN-ON SENTENCES

Do you have any run-on sentences? A run-on sentence is actually two or more sentences that run together without the proper punctuation between them. Make sure you clearly separate your ideas by clearly separating individual sentences. A comma by itself (without a conjunction like *and, but,* or *so*) is not strong enough to separate two complete ideas.

Run-on: Meet me at 2:00, I have to go over your report with you.
Correct: Meet me at 2:00. I have to go over your report with you.

Run-on: Here is the requisition form please sign at the bottom.
Correct: Here is the requisition form. Please sign at the bottom.

Run-on: I finished all of my work, I haven't started my reports.
Correct: I finished all of my work, but I haven't started my reports.

VERBS IN THE PROPER TENSE

Are your verbs in the proper tense? A very common error is shifting verb tenses, especially in reports or other communications that deal with events. Make sure you're consistent; if you're talking about something that happened in the past, all of your verbs describing that event should be in the past tense.

Inconsistent:	Mr. Turner said he wouldn't leave until he talks to Mr. Francis.
Consistent:	Mr. Turner said he wouldn't leave until he talked to Mr. Francis.

Inconsistent:	When we get back to the front desk, he decides he didn't want to wait anymore.
Consistent:	When we got back to the front desk, he decided he didn't want to wait anymore.

CHECK FOR MECHANICS

This isn't a book about mechanics, either, but a few items in this category are worth highlighting. Mechanics are such things as capitalization, punctuation, and spelling—standard practices about the presentation of words and sentences.

CAPITALIZATION

Are the proper items capitalized? The general rule is this: If you are referring to a specific person, place, or thing, the name should be capitalized. If it is a general person, place, or thing, it should not be capitalized.

Capitalized:	Our office is located on Elm Street in Williamstown.
Not capitalized:	Our office is located on a quiet street in a quiet town.

Capitalized:	I've registered for a course called New Strategies for Quality Control at Smithtown Technical College.
Not capitalized:	I've registered for a quality control class at a nearby college.

PUNCTUATION

Are sentences properly punctuated? There are many rules for punctuation, and there isn't room to go into them all here. However, a few guidelines can be found in the table below.

PURPOSE	USE
To end sentences	.
To connect complete sentences	; or , + and, or, nor, for, but, so, yet
To connect items in a list	,
To introduce a quotation	, or :
To introduce a list or explanation	:
To indicate a quotation	"
To indicate a question	?
To connect two words that are working together	- (brother-in-law)
To separate a word or phrase for emphasis	—
To separate a word or phrase that is relevant but not essential information	( )

SPELLING

Are all words spelled correctly? Have you checked for typing errors? Remember that presentation counts—and counts for a lot. Never let a communication go out with spelling or typographical errors. If you type on a computer, use the spell check, or have someone else look over your document for spelling. Even if you use spell check, look your text over—spell checks don't catch everything. You may have typed "even" instead of "seven," but because "even" is a word, the spell checker won't call that to your attention. You have to catch that error yourself.

CHECK FOR FORMAT

Again, because presentation counts, you need to be sure your communication is laid out properly on the page. Here are a few things to check for:

____ Does your document have the proper margins? One to one-and-a-half inch margins all around is standard.

____ If you're sending a letter, is your document relatively centered on the page? Avoid having too much empty white space at the top or the bottom. If your letter is short, space down a few extra lines before you begin your letter and/or add an extra space between each component.

____ Does your document have all of the parts it should have and in the order in which it should have them? Letters, memos, reports, and proposals all have specific parts that should be presented in a particular order. See Section 3 for a review.

____ Is your document printed neatly? Check that your printing ink is sharp and clear and that there aren't stray pen marks, for example, or food or drink stains on your communication before you send it out.

PRACTICE

Revise and edit the following memo. You should be able to make corrections in most of the categories above.

MEMORANDUM

TO:	John Jones, Quality Control Supervisor
FROM:	Tim
DATE:	3/10/97
RE:	Job

How are you? Fine, I hope.

Thank you for your kind letter of recommendation recommending me for the position of group leeder. Unfortunately, as you are probably already cognizant. the position was not received by me. It is my feeling that they wanted Someone with more experience. I am really down about it, but that doesn't mean I won't give it a shot next time.

Thank you again I appreciate your time and effort on my behalf.

Possible Answer to Practice Exercise

There are several problems with this memo:

1. The format of the TO/FROM lines don't match (one gives full name and title, the other just the first name).
2. The date is not written out.
3. The *re:* line is not specific enough.
4. The memo doesn't get straight to the point.
5. The sentence with "recommendation" and "recommending" has unnecessary repetition.
6. "Leeder" is spelled incorrectly.
7. "Cognizant" is pretentious language in this situation.
8. "Unfortunately, as you are probably already cognizant" is an incomplete sentence.
9. "The position was not received by me" is not an active sentence.
10. "It is my feeling that" is wordy because of the "it is" construction.

11. "They wanted" is a vague "they."

12. "Someone" should not be capitalized.

13. "Down about it" and "give it another shot" are too informal.

14. The last sentence is a run-on.

Here's one way you could correct these problems:

MEMORANDUM

TO:	John Jones, Quality Control Supervisor
FROM:	Tim Smith, Assembler
DATE:	March 10, 1997
RE:	Job Recommendation

Thank you for your kind letter recommending me for the position of group leader. Unfortunately, as you are probably already aware, I did not get the position. I believe that the production managers want someone with more experience. I am disappointed, but that doesn't mean I won't apply again next time.

Thank you again. I appreciate your time and effort on my behalf.

IN SHORT

If you want your writing to be well received, don't send it out without revising for style and editing for grammar, mechanics, and format. Check for clear, concise, complete sentences at the appropriate level of formality; correct spelling and punctuation; and the proper order of parts for your format. And don't forget that neatness counts.

Skill Building Until Next Time

Celebrate your final chapter by thinking about everything you've learned. Compare something you wrote before you started this book to something you wrote in the last few days, and then congratulate yourself on your improvement.

APPENDIX

There are lots of other books that can help you with your writing. Most of the books below focus specifically on business writing, but some are geared to almost any kind of writing. If you feel you still need to sharpen your skills after reading this book, try one of the ones listed below.

ADDITIONAL RESOURCES

Alread, Gerald, Brusaw, Charles, and Walter E. Oliu. *Writing that Works: How to Write Effectively on the Job.* 5th ed. New York: St. Martin's Press, 1995.

Bailey, Jr., Edward P. *Plain English at Work: A Guide to Writing and Speaking.* New York: Oxford University Press, 1996.

Baugh, L. Sue, Maridell Fryar, and David A. Thomas. *How to Write First-Class Business Correspondence: The Handbook for Business Writers.* Lincolnwood, IL: NTC, 1995.

Baugh, L. Sue. *How to Write First-Class Memos: The Handbook for Practical Memo Writing.* Lincolnwood, IL: NTC, 1995.

Bell, Arthur H. *Complete Business Writer's Manual: Model Letters, Memos, Reports and Presentations for Every Occasion.* Englewood Cliffs, NJ: Prentice Hall, 1991.

Bernhardt, Stephen, and Edward L. Smith. *Writing at Work: Professional Writing Skills for People on the Job.* Lincolnwood, IL: NTC, 1997.

Blake, Gary. *Quick Tips for Better Business Writing.* New York: McGraw Hill, 1995.

Blicq, Ron. *Communicating at Work: Creating Messages that Get Results.* Englewood Cliffs, NJ: Prentice Hall, 1991.

Brereton, John C., and Margaret Mansfield. *Writing on the Job.* New York: W. W. Norton & Co., 1997.

Brill, Laura. *Business Writing Quick and Easy.* New York: Amacom, 1989.

Brusaw, Charles, et al. *Handbook of Technical Writing.* 5th Ed. New York: St. Martin's Press, 1997.

Donald W. McCormick and Phyllis D. Hemphill. *Business Communication with Writing Improvement Exercises.* 5th ed. Englewood Cliffs, NJ: Prentice Hall, 1996.

Elbow, Peter. *Writing without Teachers.* New York: Oxford University Press, 1975.

Ferrara, Cosmo F. *Writing on the Job: Quick, Practical Solutions to All Your Business Writing Problems.* Englewood Cliffs, NJ: Prentice Hall, 1995.

Kolin, Philip C. *Successful Writing at Work.* 4th ed. Lexington, MA: D.C. Heath & Co., 1993.

Lauchman, Richard. *Plain Style: Techniques for Simple, Concise, Emphatic Business Writing.* New York: Amacom, 1993.

Layton, Marcia. *The Complete Idiot's Guide to Terrific Business Writing.* New York: Macmillan, 1996.

Mamchak, Steven R., Susan P. Mamchak and L. E. Frailey. *Handbook of Business Letters.* 3rd ed. Englewood Cliffs, NJ: Prentice Hall, 1991.

Pearsall, Thomas. *How to Write for the World of Work.* 5th ed. New York: Harcourt Brace, 1993.

Pitrowski, MaryAnn V. *Effective Business Writing: A Guide for Those Who Write on the Job.* New York: Harper Collins, 1996.

Poe, Roy W. The McGraw-Hill Handbook of Business Letters. 3rd ed. New York: McGraw Hill, 1994.

Prentice Hall's Get a Grip on Writing: Critical Skills for Success in Today's Business Writing. Englewood Cliffs, NJ: Prentice Hall, 1996.

Raimes, Ann. *Keys for Writers: A Brief Handbook.* Boston: Houghton Mifflin, 1996.

Reid, James, and Anne Silleck. *Better Business Letters: A Self-Instructional Book to Develop Skill in Writing.* Addison-Wesley, 1990.

Rice, Judith R. *Learning Workplace Writing.* Englewood Cliffs, NJ: Prentice Hall, 1994.

Roth, Audrey J. *The Elements of Basic Writing.* Boston: Allyn and Bacon, 1994.

Saben, Tim J. *Practical Business Communication.* Homewood, IL: Irwin Professional Publications, 1994.

Saltzman, Joel. *If You Can Talk, You Can Write: A Proven Program to Get You Writing and Keep You Writing.* New York: Warner Books, 1993.

Strunk, William, and E. B. White. *The Elements of Style.* 3rd ed. New York: Macmillan, 1979.

Stuckey, Marty. *Basics of Business Writing.* New York: Amacom Book Division, 1992.

Williams, Joseph M. *Style: Ten Lessons in Clarity and Grace.* 5th Ed. New York: Longman, 1997.

INDEX

Order Form

CALIFORNIA

___ @ $35.00   CA Police Officer
___ @ $35.00   CA State Police
___ @ $35.00   CA Corrections Officer
___ @ $20.00   CA Law Enforcement Career Guide
___ @ $35.00   CA Firefighter
___ @ $30.00   CA Postal Worker
___ @ $35.00   CA Allied Health

NEW JERSEY

___ @ $35.00   NJ Police Officer
___ @ $35.00   NJ State Police
___ @ $35.00   NJ Corrections Officer
___ @ $20.00   NJ Law Enforcement Career Guide
___ @ $35.00   NJ Firefighter
___ @ $30.00   NJ Postal Worker
___ @ $35.00   NJ Allied Health

TEXAS

___ @ $35.00   TX Police Officer
___ @ $35.00   TX State Police
___ @ $35.00   TX Corrections Officer
___ @ $20.00   TX Law Enforcement Career Guide
___ @ $35.00   TX Firefighter
___ @ $30.00   TX Postal Worker
___ @ $32.50   TX Allied Health

NEW YORK

___ @ $30.00   NYC/Nassau County Police Officer
___ @ $30.00   Suffolk County Police Officer
___ @ $30.00   NY State Police
___ @ $30.00   NY Corrections Officer
___ @ $20.00   NY Law Enforcement Career Guide
___ @ $35.00   NY Firefighter
___ @ $30.00   NY Postal Worker
___ @ $35.00   NY Allied Health

ILLINOIS

___ @ $25.00   Chicago Police Officer
___ @ $30.00   Illinois Allied Health

FLORIDA

___ @ $35.00   FL Police Officer
___ @ $35.00   FL Corrections Officer
___ @ $20.00   FL Law Enforcement Career Guide
___ @ $30.00   FL Postal Worker
___ @ $32.50   FL Allied Health

MASSACHUSETTS

___ @ $30.00   MA Police Officer
___ @ $30.00   MA State Police Exam

The MIDWEST

(Illinois, Indiana, Michigan, Minnesota, Ohio, and Wisconsin)

___ @ $30.00   Midwest Police Officer Exam
___ @ $30.00   Midwest Firefighter Exam

The SOUTH

(Alabama, Arkansas, Georgia, Louisiana, Mississippi, North Carolina, South Carolina, and Virginia)

___ @ $25.00   The South Police Officer Exam
___ @ $25.00   The South Firefighter Exam

NATIONAL EDITIONS

___ @ $14.00   Civil Service Career Starter
___ @ $12.95   Bus Operator Exam National Edition
___ @ $12.95   Sanitation Worker Exam National Edition
___ @ $12.95   U.S. Postal Service 470 Battery Exam
___ @ $14.95   Armed Services Vocational Aptitude Battery

NATIONAL STANDARDS EXAMS

___ @ $20.00   Home Health Aide National Standards Exam
___ @ $20.00   Nurse's Assistant National Standards Exam
___ @ $20.00   EMT-Basic National Standards Exam

To Order, Call TOLL-FREE: 1-888-551-JOBS, Dept. A040

Or, mail this order form with your check or money order* to:
LearningExpress, Dept. A040, 20 Academy Street, Norwalk, CT 06850

Please allow at least 2-4 weeks for delivery. Prices subject to change without notice